THE
CULTURE
OF
DEBT

How a Once-Proud Society
Mortgaged Its Future

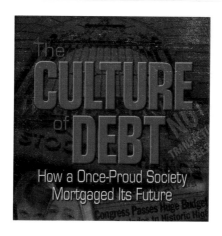

Especially for: L. Brooks Patterson

Sincerest best wishes,

THE
CULTURE
OF
DEBT

How a Once-Proud Society Mortgaged Its Future

JAMES V. McTEVIA

Afterword by David Littmann

MB Communications
Ortonville, Michigan

Manufactured in the United States of America

Cover design by Jacinta Calcut,
Image Graphics & Design, www.image-gd.com

Published by MB Communications LLC
2820 Hummer Lake Road
Ortonville, MI 48462
USA

ISBN 978-0-9845651-0-8

McTevia, James V., 1936–
    The Culture of Debt : how a once-proud society mortgaged its future / James V. McTevia ; afterword by David Littmann.
    ISBN 978-0-9845651-0-8 : $14.95
    1. Debt—United States. 2. Finance, Personal—United States.
    3. Corporate debt—United States. 4. Debts, Public—United States. I. Title.

Contents

Prologue

May 18-20, 1993

Writers are supposed to remember details such as
what the weather was like. All I remember about
the weather during my three days in Washington,
D.C., is it being far less pleasant than a visitor from
Michigan might reasonably expect in late spring.
On the other hand I vividly remember, nearly
two decades later, all those ice carts being pushed
through Capitol corridors.

My rounds began the morning of the 18th, a
Tuesday. By Thursday afternoon I had knocked on
the office door of every voting member of the United
States House and Senate. For good measure I called
on the office of Vice-President Al Gore in his capacity
as Senate tie-breaker. That's 536 doors knocked
upon. I don't know if any other citizen has ever done
this, in three days or three years. It seemed like the
most direct way of delivering my message.

Joe Knollenberg, then a Congressman from
Michigan, agreed to help me plan logistics and let
the other members of our national legislature know
I would be showing up. Some emerged for a quick
handshake; the vast majority left that to staffers.
In a few cases my reception was perceptibly cool.
Overwhelmingly, though, I was met cordially, if only
for a moment and only by staffers.

The previous year I had written a book entitled *Bankrupt: A Society Living in the Future.* You could call *Bankrupt* a "citizen book" or a "legacy book," authored by someone whose life and professional experience left him compelled to communicate a crucial message. M. Scott Peck, whose *The Road Less Traveled* also asserted that reality must be a part of the way we approach life, thought my message was so on target that he wrote the foreword to my book.

The Road Less Traveled, in my view, set the mark for explaining how all of us can live better lives with discipline and by understanding the difference between wants and needs. Dr. Peck's book sold many millions of copies and was, in fact, the best-selling self-help book ever published. *Bankrupt,* brought out by a small publisher in metropolitan Detroit where I lived and where my company still maintains an office, was never destined to be a major event in the book world. But I didn't make my trip to Washington just to sell books. I went there, on my own dime, to put a free copy of *Bankrupt* into the hands of the 536 people who could do the most to prevent the inevitable meltdown that results from mindlessly leveraging the future to serve the present.

I brought along my firm's public relations consultant and two of his young associates. All got a serious workout trying to keep up with me. We pushed dolly-loads of books down hallways, through tunnels, and onto inter-building trams. I couldn't help noting that our message wasn't the only thing being delivered to every elected official's office. Congressional employees were push-carting decanters of fresh ice water to every stop on our route. I wondered how many recipients of *Bankrupt* and icy H^2O noticed the ironic juxtaposition of private-club extravagance with my message of fiscal discipline.

On Wednesday night, with Rep. Knollenberg's help, we hosted a cocktail reception to which we invited every congressman and senator. That, we are all told, is what lobbyists do. So one could say I went to Washington as a lobbyist on behalf of future generations' security, prosperity, and happiness. I shook some more hands and talked, to anyone who would listen, about impending fiscal disaster. I don't recall exactly how many lawmakers showed up for the free drinks and to hear my message in person. I know it wasn't enough to give me laryngitis. McTevia & Associates' longtime PR consultant, the late Fred Marx, was a great friend as well as a real pro. Fred was also a most civil man. Looking back, he once described the D.C. reception as "lightly attended."

During the three days of our visit, a stringer for just one of Detroit's four TV news operations showed up to film a sound bite. Back home the *Detroit News* ran a story headlined "Mr. McTevia Goes to Washington." That was it for news media attention. We had invited them all, national and local, on grounds that private citizens—even those with expertise on a crucial topic—seldom if ever voice a public-policy concern the way I did. I thought it would make for good video as Washington news stories go. One would think a few print news outlets would have seen a human interest feature in it, regardless of my message. But the networks stayed away, the *New York Times* could not find one paragraph to spare in the nation's most complete news report, the Associated Press did not send over an intern, the *Washington Post* didn't view my visit as a unique sort of Washington story, and even Detroit media yawned. So we delivered 536 hardcover copies of *Bankrupt* and went home.

As for the mission's direct targets, just two—Rep. Tom Lewis of Florida and Vice-President Gore—responded with so much as a written note of "thanks for being a concerned citizen." This despite a good-sized work force tasked to send constituents thank-you notes, certificates of achievement, and flags that have flown above the Capitol. Maybe that kind of attention only goes to citizens certified as registered voters within a congressperson's district.

I am not whining here about the meager fruit of that 1993 Washington excursion. I am making an honest expression of amazement. Our nation was headed, my book said, toward a great fiscal train wreck. Instead of hitting the brakes, my book said, the engineer at the throttle (Congress) was pushing more and more debt into a red-hot boiler already popping its over-leveraged rivets. *Bankrupt* said we were all—citizens, government, our entire greedy culture—living a phony good life by reaching into the future and stealing our grandchildren's prosperity. Unrealistic and unsustainable debt, I said based on decades of near-unique professional experience, inevitably leads to economic catastrophe and upheaval for any individual, company, organization, government, or empire. Time to get real, I said— never a pleasant message. I certainly can't whine about Washington shooting the messenger. I merely got mortally ignored.

The calendar now reads 2010, going on two decades since my dolly-loads of books vied with ice-water carts for right-of-way in the halls of Congress. For a year and a half news media have been consumed daily by a version of the fiscal story I couldn't get anyone to talk about in 1993. Late in 2008 our society's runaway train of debt, unfunded entitlements, and endless promises of still more goodies tore around a curve leaning—from engine to caboose—within an inch of tipping into a bottomless fiscal gorge. Many or most of the world's economies stood a good chance of being dragged onto the same debris heap. In short, the message of *Bankrupt* had proved on target. The subprime mortgage collapse and ensuing Great Recession only scratched the surface of our Debt Disaster, but it was a scratch felt around the world.

Unfortunately, another part of *Bankrupt*'s message has also proved true. Debt-addicted individuals and institutions, given half a chance or less, will keep borrowing money and live further into the future than even science fiction could predict. Contemporary society's punch-drunk capacity to avoid fiscal reality by robbing future generations is an awesome thing. It appears possible the most powerful nation on Earth will find ways to loot the future all the way into our *great-great*-grandchildren's bank accounts before we come to our senses—voluntarily or otherwise—about discipline and the ultimate need to repay what we borrow. Meanwhile, the intricate global nature of this house of credit cards only intensifies.

Tracing the linkage bears worrisome similarity to the way an obscure archduke's assassination a century ago led to what was supposed to be The War to End All Wars.

I am worried as a person can be on behalf of future generations. I think I am eminently qualified to tell you that the disastrous results of crippling, unsustainable debt cannot be prevented by incurring still more crippling, unsustainable debt. One would think common sense would make credentialing unnecessary. Our Debt Disaster's madness compares with nothing so well as the Cold War's mad race to stockpile more and more nuclear weapons when we already had ability to vaporize the planet many times over.

So here I am with another manuscript written from my perspective—now more than half a century's worth—as a professional observer, analyzer, and repairer of debt-driven disasters. I never thought I'd scribble words onto the pages of a book again, and I definitely have no plans of lugging 536 copies down to Washington. Back in 1993 I held a reasonable amount of optimism. This time around I feel like I am shouting "Watch out!" to a citizenry at whom a bullet already has been fired, as if either common sense or professional experience can somehow intercept and knock down a chunk of hot lead that has all our names on it. But one must shout anyway. Besides, an immediate return to fiscal reality and sanity might mean America could escape this mess while enduring nothing worse than a little social upheaval and some very serious pain.

In truth I believe we—our leaders and us—will not summon the courage and belated discipline to escape so easily. I could be wrong. Everything in my professional experience tells me I am entirely correct. By the time this book is in your hands you already will have heard endless discussion and posturing about our Debt Disaster. Trust me, any worst-case scenario you hear might be an understatement. Our way of life is in jeopardy. At least several future generations might never even get a chance to taste prosperity, or even security. All because they were asked to settle a very, very large tab run up by their elders. Shame on us.

For Jason, Jocelyn, Maggie, Nathan, Nicole,
Jenna, Jacob and Madison

My Grandchildren

—Gramps

1

The Leveraged Life

People seemed to be content.
Fifty dollars paid the rent.
Freaks were in a circus tent.
Those were the days.
> —*All in the Family* theme song.

I want it all.
I want it all.
I want it all.
And I want it now.
> —Queen.

Millions of viewers who tuned in America's top-rated TV show on March 8, 1975, saw Archie and Edith Bunker do something that was, as usual for them, out of touch with the times. The Bunkers hosted a mortgage-burning party. By 1975 the idea of paying off a home mortgage—commonplace in a fiscally sane society just two decades earlier—already had become a rare sight. In 1945 the wave of World War II veterans returning from Europe or the Pacific found civilian jobs, saved a chunk of their paycheck until they could pay 20 percent down, then bought houses realistically matched to their incomes. They commonly made double payments each month to get out from under their mortgage as soon as possible. The day they set ablaze a piece of paper representing their biggest debt was one of the happiest moments of their lives.

By the '90s most loan officers could not remember a homeowner hosting a mortgage-burning party. Many in the new generation had never heard of such a thing and couldn't imagine why anyone would celebrate being out of debt. The new lender's job description called for selling home "owners" a "re-fi" as soon as the client accumulated enough equity to start all over by turning it into more debt. In earlier generations, taking on a major debt obligation meant a hat-in-hand trip to the bank to ask for a loan. Now it became a telemarketing business where lenders went out and pitched customers, who were all too eager to oblige. Millions of borrowers went to the trough repeatedly. A CitiBank advertisement cheered them on: "There's got to be at least $25,000 hidden in your house. We can help you find it."

Who would have thought Archie's and Edith's quaint attitude toward debt could help us understand fundamental social change, and help us fathom the source of so much current anxiety and future misery? Who would have thought, for that matter, that a goliath like CitiBank could plunge below $1 a share as the 2009 crisis of confidence rocked Wall Street? Who can doubt that any turnaround will be a mirage until debt-addicted America re-establishes contact with fiscal reality? Well, me, for one. Not that I possess better vision than others. It's the vantage point that matters, and for 50 years I've had the clearest possible view of our oncoming fiscal train wreck. By that I mean the Big One, not the fender-bender we just had as the Great Recession got under way. Bad as things looked in early 2009, *far* worse things than the failure of a few global corporations lie ahead if we don't reconnect with basic financial truths. Here's a scary fact: Elected leaders of the United States and the titans of Wall Street do not understand, prescribe, or practice fiscal sanity as well as Archie and Edith Bunker did.

As for those four lines from the British band Queen—including "I want it all!" repeated three times like a spoiled child's rant in a toy store—who would have thought a rock anthem would precisely and succinctly point to where our society went wrong? Two wicked bits of irony: one major retail corporation that used Queen's song in a TV commercial wound up in bankruptcy, never to emerge. Another corporation thought "I want it all" was the perfect jingle for a financial institution. The latter corporation was among those heavily damaged by an appetite for "toxic" mortgage derivatives. That kind of investment, of course, would have been Greek not only to the Bunkers, but to every Wall Street guru in Archie and Edith's heyday. Things didn't just change; they changed incredibly fast, like making a U-turn on a drag strip.

One moment Americans were living a fiscally sane life, within our means and very much in the present rather than leveraged deep into an unknowable future. The next moment, it seems, America lost contact with financial reality. The houses we live in illustrate the change perfectly. If a post-World War II bungalow somehow could make its way into a subdivision filled with 21st Century McMansions, it would look like a homesteader cabin awaiting demolition. Back in 1950 the vast majority of the world's population would have loved to live in that bungalow. That's still true. Americans, though, began demanding ever-bigger houses whether they could afford them or not. Mortgage-burning parties became sitcom fare. Many millions of Americans wanted it *all* and wanted it *now*. They looked around the present and didn't see any way to buy the things they wanted—not just larger houses but cars and gadgets and toys in mindless profusion. Consumers moved their lives into the future by "spending" all the *debt* they could find. First they raided cash from their own futures, pretending that tomorrow could only be ever-more-prosperous. Our society got into the habit of living high ("Live richly," was the tag line of that CitiBank campaign) with no basis except grotesque optimism. One rosy cornerstone was the idea of living several years in a house owned almost entirely by a bank, then selling the house for enough money to pay off the mortgage, pay a realtor's commission, ship the furnishings across country —and still show enough profit to start the cycle all over again. In a bigger house, of course.

Meanwhile, our institutions and our government locked themselves onto that same misguided beacon

—living beyond their means, reaching into the future, and burdening unborn generations with someone else's debt. Cautionary advice about such generational theft is, and has been, out there for all to see and hear. I find little evidence our society has paid any meaningful attention. Very few Americans seem to realize the scope of our debt disaster and how close we are to total, possibly fatal immersion in it. Not even the Great Recession has managed to inspire genuine interest. Not if understanding a problem that threatens our entire society means taking the most basic step toward solving it. Americans, their institutions, and their government have jumbo mortgaged this country's future. Worse, it's a subprime mortgage. The balloon payment lurking around the corner will be a day of reckoning unlike anything ever seen in world financial history.

In this big picture of mindless, crushing, hopelessly unrealistic levels of debt I can see just one honest reason for hope. That is, we know fiscal *sanity* once was the norm. It is a provable fact that men and women used to live happily and successfully in the present rather than trying to buy it all, right now, on an unrealistic promise to pay, somehow, in the future. Honest. A few creatures from such an era still walk the Earth. And many of today's young people understand these truths better than elders who wandered off into the future to harvest fool's gold. Are too few fiscally sane young Americans arriving on the scene, and too late? We shall see.

The U.S. government has dug itself into a hole so deep it came out in China and the vicinity. Beijing leads the world in lending U.S. dollars back to the country that printed them. Japan ranks a close second. At this writing, the U.S.—you and I, but mostly our descendants—owe $800 billion to China, with the total borrowed from Japan also approaching a trillion dollars. Exactly how much future cash we have pledged to pay altogether, in what form, and to whom, will be a later topic. (The $13 trillion on the official national-debt meter as these words go into print is only about one-fourth of Washington's looming financial obligation, as measured the way a company would legally be bound to measure it). We sail steadily on course to deepen that world-record money pit by huge amounts...assuming the market for full faith and credit in our heavily mortgaged future doesn't finally collapse. Our sovereign debt held by China, Japan and other governments is a sort of national charge card, representing actual dollars we are pledged to pay. But Washington has other ways of raiding the future, meaning those T-bills and such are sort of a petty-cash way of staying liquid even as we march toward insolvency. Meanwhile, interest rate uncertainties leave Uncle Sam in the same dicey situation as anyone whose life is wrecked by a credit-card company moving rates upward a few points.

That's just a simple glance at debt ledgers without trying to assess and include the complexities of, say, Chinese goods pouring onto the shelves of Wal-Mart. The private sector sending dollars out of the country to buy things, and our government borrowing piles of those dollars right back to keep its own "I want it all" ethic afloat, has been our national pastime for quite a while.

If that sounds like a Ponzi scheme, that's because it *is* a Ponzi scheme. It makes Bernie Madoff's swindle look like a misdemeanor. The Land of the Free and the Home of the Brave has been borrowing money to pay interest on money it has already borrowed. In amounts defying comprehension. With our government's engagement in military conflict and potential conflict around the globe, with Washington's endless appetite for new spending obligations, and Congress's total distaste for paying the tab on programs that already exist, plus the impending explosion in unfunded Social Security and Medicare/Medicaid due bills, this national Ponzi scheme would be in danger of crumbling in the best of times. As we all painfully know, this is *not* the best of times—economic recovery or no economic recovery. Exotic and just plain silly debt that flourished to fuel the "I want it all" lifestyle precipitated our current short-term earthquake but, more importantly, our long-term quagmire. Nonetheless, as has been the norm for half a century, it appears we will attempt to dodge pain and fiscal reality by *borrowing still more money*. We are so very, very far from having a national mortgage-burning party that I despair whether that happy occasion can occur in my *great*-grandchildren's lifetimes, even if we try to make it happen.

Why in the world did we let debt service creep toward becoming the core item on our national agenda? And why, after watching the ugly result, does our government seem to think it can dig us out by spending still more money it does not have? We have allowed America's tradition of "every generation 'living better' than the previous generation" to go in the tank faster than you can say "bankrupt." How can we expect coming generations to look back at us with anything but disdain, at best? Respect for elders is about to take the biggest, and most deserving, hit in recorded history.

I've been working with dollar numbers and debt all my adult life. For a little more than three decades I have worked with *big* dollar numbers and *big* debt. But even I do not easily comprehend "million with a 'b' instead of an 'm'." Now Americans from every walk of life are being asked, as nonchalantly as one might swipe a credit card at a McDonald's drive-through, to comprehend "billion with a 'tr' instead of a 'b'." Most Americans and their leaders seem to be responding: "No big deal. No problem." There is... trust me on this...a direct connection between using plastic to buy a fast-food hamburger and spending a few *trillion* dollars you don't have. But the prevailing "wisdom" seems to be saying: "Hey, it's not money, it's only debt. Have a burger."

My despair about this tragicomedy is as selfish as it gets, but not for my own creature comforts. A lifetime of hard work and good fortune have taken care of that, although I hope to keep that good life as good as possible by never retiring. As I enter my 70s I am busier in my profession than I was 20 years ago. But I worry every day about prospects for the line of humanity that began—or rather, continued—with my wife and me. Like most people, we envision our line extending, and thriving, as far as the eye can see and beyond. We have children. They have children. With a little luck we will live to see a further generation take root. Will our society stop stealing from its young and from the yet-unborn before it's too late for *them* and *their children* to craft a good life, or even a decent life, let alone a better life? The current economic morass eventually might stop the runaway train, however painfully. Or maybe we will somehow stumble through the crisis and just keep swiping our plastic through the card-reader. In that case someone will have to tell us what comes next after millions, billions, and trillions. And somewhere out ahead, around another curve, one generation or another will get run over by this freight train of debt. It *will* happen. The longer we let the train run away, the worse the big wreck is going to be.

I want my grandkids and their kids to know how several generations of their forebears insisted on living in the future, and how I saw this happening from both a professional and personal perspective. I want them to know that their grandfather and great-grandfather was one of those who foresaw the inevitable result and that I shouted warnings every time I had a chance, and that any such warnings were regarded as quainter than Archie and Edith's mortgage-burning party. That's why if no one reads these chapters but my own family and a few friends, my first purpose in writing this book will have been served. If others read it, that's frosting on a cash-and-carry cake. There's a phrase—"cash and carry" —that almost every living American has either not heard in a long time, or has *never* heard. That's not a quaint fact. It's a sad fact. Handy, though, in explaining what went wrong in our society, and how "generation theft" took hold.

Probably the best place to start is to devote the rest of this chapter to reminding and illustrating that once upon a time (it does indeed sound like fable from long, long ago) this society did *not* live in the future by spending resources it did not have and had no prospect of acquiring any time soon, if ever. We are not talking ancient history. The bad stuff began in my lifetime. In fact, the bad stuff didn't begin until I entered adulthood. I was born in 1936. The first generation defined by debt came on the scene, trying to leverage life instead of living it, around the time I entered the job market after high school. It took me a little while to recognize what was happening. I myself spent a few years living in the future so I could support a young family that went from two members to six in just four years. But let's first go back to a time before even a dinosaur like me walked the Earth.

World War I ended in 1918. The last surviving combat veterans of this "War to End All Wars" died only recently. The Great Depression—a world "war" of a different sort—began in 1929 and didn't end until World War II began. A few "veterans" of the Great Depression therefore remain with us, but they are elderly and their number dwindles rapidly. I barely can remember, around age three at the end of that economic nightmare, door-to-door beggars seeking food.

The desperation and, at the same time, the resourcefulness and *pride* of the Great Depression generation can be found in the very fine 2005 movie *Cinderella Man*. The film is based on the life and career of boxer Jim Braddock, who won the light heavyweight championship one year before my birth. His desperation to put food on the table, the pain of moving his family from a comfortable home to a cold-water flat (and finding rent money to stay in the flat), was reality for millions of Americans during the Depression. So was the pride that accompanied their cash-and-carry lifestyle. Not everyone could, like Jim Braddock, translate desperation and pride into a boxing career so unlikely that newspaperman Damon Runyon coined the "Cinderella Man" nickname. But the national will to "get by" was enormous. It had to be.

In 1933, for instance, one in four Americans who wanted to work could not find a job. That's about three times the early-2009 unemployment rate which led to several trillion dollars worth of "economic stimulus" and corporate bailout packages and new federal spending (all, of course, on credit). In 1933, besides the millions of unemployed, millions more found themselves reduced to part-time work in jobs below their former station. In the four years after 1929, per-capita income in the U.S. fell from $700 per year to $400 (a dollar certainly was a dollar then). Looking at that 43 percent plunge in *average* income, keep in mind that some Americans were doing quite well despite it all. The '30s, after all, were the classic years for Duesenbergs and

Cords, and for Hollywood glamour. The disparity between that kind of wealth and the millions of ordinary workers and farmers who hit rock bottom accounts for the "mere" 43 percent reversal of fortune. It was, in so many fundamental respects, an entirely different America.

Comprehensive health-care insurance was not an issue in 1933, even for the privileged. Blue Cross was in the process of being invented. Medicare and Medicaid did not exist (and would not until 1965). Depression-era Americans reached into their wallets and purses to pay for doctor visits or house calls. And for a time after World War II one might witness a scene in a town park where a retiring doctor was handed the keys to a new car by a crowd of his loving patients—many of whom once paid for a child's tonsillectomy with fresh produce grown in their backyard. By 2010 that kind of doctor/patient relationship was fodder for TV comedians and rarer than house calls.

About 9,000 U.S. banks closed during the Depression, 4,000 in just the first few months of 1933. When President Franklin D. Roosevelt took office, his first acts included declaring a series of "bank holidays" to head off runs on deposits, and shepherding a series of new banking laws into existence—chiefly creating the Federal Deposit Insurance Corporation.

Cars? Many families in the heartland did have one, and if the owner was lucky enough to keep his job he likely kept his car. But the two-car garage was reserved for the affluent class. Even in small towns and rural America many did not own even one set of wheels, at least not motorized wheels. In the great cities, cars were a luxury. If you needed to get somewhere, you took a streetcar or the el train. If you had a few bucks, you hailed a cab. For sure, people *walked* a whole lot more than today. You will not find much obesity, let alone an epidemic of fat, in the images from those days. If you lived in urban America and had a car, you probably were wealthy, or near it.

Hopes and dreams—and the ideal of every American generation being better off than the previous one? Our Depression-era forebears not only didn't buy unnecessary goods they couldn't pay for, to a significant extent they didn't have *children* they couldn't pay for. For the first time in American history, the birth rate fell below replacement level.

Pop songs? Keep Queen's greedy ditty in mind as you read Yip Harburg's mournful lyrics for the runaway hit of 1932, popular in two different recordings, by Bing Crosby and Rudy Vallee. It could not possibly be further removed from "I want it all. And I want it now." Harburg's words resonated with millions of American listeners who knew firsthand the pain he was talking about:

> *They used to tell me I was building a dream*
> *And so I followed the mob*
> *When there was earth to plow or guns to bear*
> *I was always there right on the job*
> *They used to tell me I was building a dream*
> *With peace and glory ahead*

Why should I be standing in line
Just waiting for bread?
Once I built a railroad, I made it run
Made it race against time
Once I built a railroad, now it's done
Brother, can you spare a dime?
Once I built a tower up to the sun
Brick and rivet and lime
Once I built a tower, now it's done
Brother, can you spare a dime?

We can't get a full sense of that time and place by listening to "Brother, Can You Spare a Dime," or by watching *Cinderella Man*, or by looking square into the weary and frightened eyes staring back from photos shot in the rural Dust Bowl or on the urban bread lines. But the lyrics and the images help us see the pain that fell on Americans from coast to coast. We know countless lives were broken by that pain. But we also know millions—not just a few Cinderella men and women—emerged from the pain to build a better society. The 16 million Americans who took a side trip to wear a uniform during the most cataclysmic war in world history have been dubbed—with few voices raised in serious dispute—our "Greatest Generation." Younger Americans who rightfully expressed wonderment at the terrible images in *Saving Private Ryan* need to know, too, about the economic war that preceded the shooting war. The character and courage the Greatest Generation demonstrated in battle is all the more astounding when one realizes that millions of Americans went off to serve—

and in 291,000 cases to die for—a nation in which a spare dime might have made a day's difference.

Obviously, these two defining events of the 20th Century—the Depression and World War II—are joined at the hip. For any American who experienced one or the other, it is the thing that shaped his or her life. Any American who was on the front lines of *both* the economic collapse and the shooting war is someone who endured far, far more than any of us since then can imagine. Most of the people we entrusted with governing the country and shaping our policies for four decades after WWII were people who had experienced the Depression or the war at some level. Somehow, despite those modest post-war homes and those double payments and those mortgage-burning parties and that generation's foursquare response to crisis and pain, those four post-war decades are when we revved up what I regard as America's third defining event of the 20th Century. Unfortunately, there is nothing noble about this event, which unfortunately has reached into the 21st Century with no end in sight.

I refer, of course, to our mushroom cloud of debt—a cloud which, come to think of it, would be the perfect graphic for Queen's lyrics. What is the half-life of a debt measured in trillions of dollars, anyway? How many generations have we poisoned so far? What is more "now" than a mushroom cloud? My figurative questions are not meant in any way to belittle the real threat of a real mushroom cloud. If we had to trade one mushroom cloud for the other, it would be an obvious choice. Luckily for sound fiscal policy, that's a choice there is no point in making. Either mushroom cloud could reduce our society to rubble, though in vastly different ways. Nice if we could do away with both threats.

I am not an economist and I am not a historian. So I won't try to explain the causes of the Great Depression, or the causes of World War II. I won't try to blame generational theft on the Greatest Generation—though it is tempting to link the deprivations of depression and war with the desire to have "the good life" at all costs. But the returning troops (and profiteers on the home front) did not charge into indebted chaos the day Japan surrendered in 1945. Those modest post-war homes and modest mortgages *were* the norm. If you walked up to the average citizen in 1948 and asked if his car loan was longer-term or shorter-term than average, he might well have told you he paid cash. If he asked what the typical length of a car loan was, and you told him five years (as it is today), he would take you to be a mental-ward escapee. Twenty percent was standard for a home down payment, and would remain so for several decades. Paying cash for a car was common, paying a third or more down and financing for just one year or—gasp!—18 months was typical. Across the breadth of consumer wants and needs, that kind of fiscal sanity was standard operating procedure.

Did you have your eye on a new coat at the local department store? Fine. Go to the Layaway Department, give them a few bucks, and they'll hold it for you until you have enough cash to buy it. (Note to young readers: I am not making this up. You've heard of those wild and crazy '60s? Stores still had layaway departments. You could have a few Beatles albums "put on layaway" if you wished.)

Use your plastic? Major gasoline companies were already issuing credit cards to preferred customers —but the cards could not be used to buy other goods, and the user had to pay the full amount when billed. Some retailers also issued their cards for use only at their own stores. The war had been over for five years before the Diners Club card arrived on the scene, in 1950, allowing businessmen and others to charge meals at any participating restaurant (but again the cardholder had to pay up in full when billed—meaning these were "charge cards," not "credit cards"—and he could not go across the street after dinner and use the card to buy a new radio).

American Express and Bank of America issued their first credit cards in 1958, just one year before NBC began broadcasting *Bonanza* in "Living Color." That meant widespread means of living every day deeper into debt, plus a supercharged means for retailers to entice the populace into doing so, had come to town on the same bus. Our finances were indeed headed south, and quickly; but it's worth noting that the war had been over for 13 years. People my age—just nine years old when WWII ended—were into their 20s, into their cars, into the workplace, and not about to be denied the right to do things that were new and stupid.

My own relationship to the new order in personal finance was unusual. I have always enjoyed spending money, and spend it I did. But it was real money, not charge slips. I was fortunate to have family connections in the Great Lakes freighter fleet, and I shipped out to spend a summer below decks as a coal handler when I was 14. I have no idea how many laws that would break today, but back then it meant I was making more money than my father. I did this every summer through high school. It allowed me to be the biggest spender in my small high school in Marine City, Michigan, for sure. I *did* enjoy the clothes and wheels and toys of teenagehood like few working-class kids of the '50s could. Still, I didn't go into debt. And if I was tempted to stay a full season on the lake boats and become truly "rich," that was where the goose with the golden egg set her foot down. I was told I had to go to high school. So my life pattern was set: want it all, go for it all, take all you can get, but first get cash to pay for it.

For just a couple years I found out what it was like to live in the future. My new and rapidly growing family was buried in debt almost as quickly as we could say thank you for the wedding gifts. It wasn't clothes and vacations and toys and such that had me suffocating in debt even while I worked as a young repo man, going into the dead of night to retrieve Crown Victorias whose owners had stepped too far into the financial future. It was doctor bills and hospital bills, this being the tail end of that part of history where one was expected to pay for these things out of pocket. My personal debt was still hanging over my head when I left the repo job and moved up to a bank's commercial loan department. If nothing makes a good loan officer better than possessing first-hand knowledge of what "overextended" means, then I definitely hit the bank floor running. That's where I began to understand the truths I am trying to convey here.

By the time I launched my own business helping troubled companies recover and survive, my personal financial life was securely anchored in the present. I was, however, approaching 20/20 vision in seeing the toxic nature of debt. By the time I helped invent "turnaround management" and served as a bankruptcy receiver (and, after a change in the law, as a bankruptcy trustee) on scores of sad cases that ruined the lives of thousands, I had X-ray vision when it comes to seeing the ultimate cause of so much misery. So, yes, debt lies at the center of what you will be reading here. Debt is the bad guy in the tale, and not an imaginary one. I've seen this villain's work up close. Debt has been the driving force at virtually every wrong turn taken by my clients. Debt has been in *total* control at every dead end. That's not "simplistic." That's simply fact.

We are not, with rare exception, talking about people who are not smart. Quite the opposite. The debt culture that took root in the late '50s meant even smart people began using credit to buy trifles and began signing big personal debt obligations they should not have signed. It also meant they took that debt culture into their small businesses and major board rooms and law firms—and then into elective office. In the debt culture for a dime, in for a dollar. Or millions of dollars. Next thing you know it's 2010, the meter is still running, and you are talking trillions of dollars. Double-digit trillions.

In retrospect, I'd love to be able to point a finger square at the culprit, to make positive identification of who or what opened this Pandora's Box as I entered adulthood. I don't think that can be done. If anybody could have been expected to lead the charge straight into a debt disaster it would be that wave of war veterans. It didn't happen that way. A lot of temptations came on the scene at one time, as that timeline regarding credit cards and color TV illustrates. It had to be even more complex, though. Some of it must relate to the one word that keeps coming to mind as I try to put the pieces of that time and place back together: "loose." Credit wasn't the only thing that loosened in those days. Our society, for better or worse—or for better *and* worse—threw overboard so many strictures and boundaries and caveats and "morals" (as behavioral ideals were commonly called) that if there were such a profession as "social accountant," no ledger book would be large enough to catalogue the changes.

The '50s were when television took over, meaning modern cathode ray tube media, racing along a timeline that reaches from black and white network shows, to color broadcasts, to 100-channel cable systems, to video games in which 12-year-olds win points by committing violent if merely virtual crimes, to computers and even cell phones that eventually would deliver all media via one portal.

As for the *content* of so much media, did a guy in Chicago with a smoking jacket and a tobacco pipe really, all by himself, change *that* much about

America? It seems doubtful. But Hugh Hefner's first issue of Playboy in 1953 is as good an icon as any to hang on the wall when pointing to a society that one night, so to speak, went to bed as Puritans and woke up as hedonists. One minute neither an actor nor an actress could disrobe on screen, and the actor had to keep at least one foot on the floor. The next minute they could have sex on screen, and with a little technological ingenuity a 10-year-old could watch.

I like contemporary movies when they're done well (I watch them often, and I've already touted one here). Obviously I didn't switch radio stations when Queen came on the air. I am not a foot soldier for any neo-Puritan movement. I don't see any value in championing uptight morals for the sake of uptight morals. It's the culture of debt that I know something about, and that is the subject that concerns me. But it's very, very difficult to look back on how *everything* changed, including our attitude toward theft from future generations, and not wonder exactly what that stew's active ingredient might have been. It began simmering in the '50s and got to boiling in the '60s—when it gave us not just Woodstock but the government handbook on how to create domestic programs without funding them. I don't know where it all came from, but "the loosening of America" wouldn't be a bad theory.

No matter, really. I don't care how you regard contemporary American art and entertainment when you finish reading this book. But I hope, for the sake of my descendants and yours, that sharing my professional vantage point and my experiences will have serious effect on the way you regard our debt culture. Either mushroom cloud, the figurative or the literal, might kill us. If I were the wagering kind, I know which one I would put my money on as most likely to be fully unleashed.

One disclaimer: If you perceive a single word of partisan politics in this book, it is entirely an accident. I am the most apolitical person you will meet this week. Everything I say about politicians and debt could be ascribed to either major party. I invite them both—in a colloquialism that says it perfectly—to get real.

2

Free and Clear

That was the biggest American financial lesson the Icelanders took to heart: the importance of buying as many assets as possible with borrowed money, as asset prices only rose. By 2007, Icelanders owned roughly 50 times more foreign assets than they had in 2002.

— Michael Lewis, writing in the April 2009 *Vanity Fair* magazine after Iceland's banks, government, and citizens all crashed into bankruptcy.

Congress is poised to miss its April 15 deadline for finishing next year's budget without even considering a draft in either chamber. Unlike citizens' tax-filing deadline, Congress's mid-April benchmark is nonbinding. And members seem in no rush to get the process going.

Indeed, some Democratic insiders suspect that leaders will skip the budget process altogether this year—a way to avoid voting on spending, deficits, and taxes in an election year—or simply go through the motions without any real effort to complete the work.

— *Politico*, April 12, 2010.

America unquestionably has inspired much good in this world. Also, unfortunately, we have inspired much that is bad. Just ask the Icelanders. In 2007 the United Nations ranked Iceland, population 310,000, as the top country on the Human Development Index. That's a complex statistical attempt to measure freedom, productivity, life expectancy, educational levels, cultural resources, and GDP per capita. True, Iceland's endless winter nights can generate melancholy. Consider, though, that the island's entire supply of heat to keep dwellings and offices comfortable until summer is piped from limitless underground geothermal sources. On balance, Iceland must have been destined, as the United Nations suggested, to be a contented society.

Well, the Icelanders once *were* a happy, or at least contented, bunch. Then a few years ago this thrifty, successful crew of cod fishermen and their land-based support staff discovered how to steal American-style from their grandchildren. Icelanders tried to leverage themselves out of their long winter and into an allegedly better life. Iceland's banks bought into the worst Wall Street schemes. The man on the Icelandic street maxed out his plastic, began coveting the Arctic version of a McMansion, and even took to playing the world currency market. Not to be outdone in the arena of exotic finances, Icelanders linked currency speculation to their SUV purchases. A vehicle would be bought with a particular currency in hope it would float upward against the Icelandic krona, dropping the car's cost.

Icelanders forgot that the core source of their perch atop the UN Human Development Index lay in chasing cod through frigid waters. Take your eye off the cod and nasty things happen.

Less than a year after being honored as the most solid nation on Earth, Iceland went bust. The banking system collapsed. Iceland's per-capita national debt soared to three times that of the U.S. The government was tossed from office. Serious discussion about replacing Iceland's plummeting krona with the euro was followed by a U.K-Dutch bailout of Iceland's banks. It only took a few billion dollars to do the job, but keep in mind that nearly three times as many people live within Detroit's city limits as live in all of Iceland. Early in 2010 the new Icelandic government proposed garnisheeing Icelanders' paychecks an average $135 a month for eight years to help pay back the Brits and Dutch. The idea of actually repaying sovereign debt was put to a national referendum, and more than 90 percent of Icelanders voted against it. When was the last time you saw any free-world electorate vote 9-to-1 on the same side of *anything*? Iceland's binge of borrowing, speculating, and borrowing to speculate some more, and then owing lots of money for failed speculations and unpaid debts, might sound familiar. In any case, it caused profound misery in what used to be regarded as the top of the world in more ways than just ice cover.

All very interesting, though a long way from Main Street U.S.A. But only on a map. Iceland crashed because it became more American than fast food. World politics are not my specialty, but the Iceland story caught my attention in an instant. One doesn't often, after all, see an entire nation go into receivership. Besides, the tiny island nation's insolvency became the global cutting edge of 21st Century sovereign debt nightmares. It took only a matter of months for Greece to join the parade, leaving a much larger tab to be paid. Other Euro countries instantly began flirting with their own days of reckoning. As this book went to press, the European Union itself was staggering under its debt load, with global implications. In May 2010, as United Kingdom voters tossed out *their* government, the BBC reported analysts estimating a genuine solution to Britain's debt disaster would require sending home 500,000 government workers. Population-adjusted, that would be 2,500,000 government workers in the United States. The next steps—or dominos— were yet to be resolved. Needless to say it has been interesting to watch other nations, of whatever size, approach and even cross the red line that my 1992 book said will bring even America to its knees if it does not put its fiscal house in order.

It's best not to try forecasting these things with any precision. Runaway debt kills with great certainty but not on a neatly predictable schedule. What is known at this writing is that very unpleasant circumstances already have befallen Icelanders and Greeks, have shaken European capitals, and given nervous hits to equity markets worldwide. That's enough to illustrate an audacious fact I reported to you in Chapter One. It no doubt sounded like a figure of speech, but I mean it literally. Using your credit card to buy a bag of hamburgers is an individual act of fiscal insanity that staggers in lockstep to a government's insane decision to write trillion-dollar checks when it is already 10 trillion dollars in the hole. You *will* be sent a bill for that bag of burgers. You *will* be billed for that trillion dollars. And unless you are a truly heartless sort, you *will* be ashamed when you finally understand and admit you must pass that debt—plus interest—to your kids and their kids.

Individual behavior does matter. It is the thread of our social fabric. We are the sum of you and I. That is not just a quaint notion out of some star-spangled feel-good Frank Capra movie. The behavior of individuals, and families, and neighborhoods, and cities, and each incrementally larger group is all of one piece. That is even more so today, when you can communicate instantaneously—and make instantaneous toxic financial decisions—from anywhere via your laptop or Blackberry. If it takes a couple hundred thousand Icelanders going off a fiscal cliff to make the point... well, it is tragic for Iceland but we should not let the example go to waste. The *Vanity Fair* writer who traveled to Reykjavik heard occasional explosions from outside his hotel room. Inquiry revealed the noise was a then commonplace sound: SUVs being blown up by their owners. Their large new toys had gone underwater—not in the north Atlantic, but in the sense that they were worth less than the amount owed—and each blast signaled an insurance claim. Perhaps never in the history of runaway consumer debt has there been such an apt metaphor, let alone

one so—*boom!*—vivid. Top-to-bottom and bottom-to-top all tapped out. An entire country vertically integrated into its kids' piggy banks.

I have never—thank you very much—been called upon to straighten out the financial affairs of an entity that has, literally, the power to print money. Not even an entity as small, relatively speaking, as Iceland. Printing money is, however, the *only* means of going into debt not used by one or another of my clients in driving themselves so far south financially as to need help salvaging—or liquidating—what once had been a good and profitable idea. If companies were ranked on some index the way the U.N. once ranked a solvent Iceland on top, many of my client firms and bankruptcy cases also could have pointed proudly to *their* years on top. The level of debt-driven damage I have discovered in formerly exemplary businesses has ranged from stifling (best-case scenario) to fatal (hundreds of those; and though some were in much worse shape than others, "fatal" is, well, fatal). I shudder to imagine how much further some of these companies could have lived into the future if they had printing presses capable of spraying out pallet-loads of $100 bills at no cost except paper and ink.

But before moving on to discuss economic suicide committed by companies and organizations and governments accumulating indebtedness ranging from huge to incomprehensible, let's focus this chapter on individuals and families. Let's take a good look at financial clarity and sanity down at the personal level before we tackle groups and bigger groups and the biggest group of all. Let's start where even the most messed-up finances don't involve the word "trillion" or even "billion." Let's illustrate that straight-line connection from bottom to top and top to bottom. Just like Iceland.

In my long career dealing with troubled companies—large, small, industrial, retail—it always has been the people and their circumstances, much more so than the businesses themselves, that stay in my mind long after I move on to the next client. My firm is hired to do what needs to be done to make a troubled company's balance sheet whole, not to repair the personal finances of the company's principals. But connect the dots and guess what? That's right. One rarely examines a troubled set of corporate books without seeing troubled personal finances all around the periphery.

When meeting with companies' principals to bring them bad news, I've never heard overleveraged Land Rovers exploding in the parking lot. What I and my firm's associates *do* routinely hear is just as dramatic but more subtle, like a stage play rather than an action movie. Audible gasps. The sound of someone swallowing hard (I have actually *heard* that). Faint involuntary groans. I speak straightforwardly and look the clients in the eye; but often enough they will stare over my shoulder into some imaginary zone where the books still balance and the country club membership is not evaporating.

So even without getting involved in a client's personal lives and finances, this supposedly cold and arm's-length profession of mine can, and usually does, become a personal thing. What a client sees in that imaginary zone over my shoulder very often is the end of something that has meant the good life for several generations, and many branches, of a family. This place where individual threads are woven together in a business is an important swatch of the social fabric. When I sew up a threadbare patch as best as possible, if possible, I'm doing work that would not have been necessary if owners and managers themselves had been willing, earlier, to hear and confront what their balance sheet was saying.

I began seeing this pattern of avoidance and denial mirrored in principals' personal finances way back when there was no McTevia & Associates, just this one McTevia branching out from my youthful days as a bank loan officer to do free-lance consultant work. In those early times, client companies did not engage my services to resolve their own debt problems but to deal with customers who owed *them* money. Which is exactly what I did at the bank—identify customers whose loans were shifting to the problem side, and solve the bank's problem. You see how it wasn't such a long stretch from my very earliest working days as a car repo man to working in a bank's commercial loan department. It seems, in fact, that all across a financial career that has culminated in some very interesting decades in some high-powered places, after some bottom-rung beginnings, debt has been the active ingredient of every task. That includes going up a blind alley to recover a car whose "owner" was 120 days overdue, to helping stabilize the financial world of an honored philanthropist who is about to watch the family business slide into receivership.

When I first started working with commercial clients, several offices of the National Association of Credit Management (NACM), a trade group of commercial credit executives with chapters across the country, offered "adjustment" services. If a member company had a problem collecting from a customer, that debtor customer would be "adjusted." This meant making the debtor a settlement offer he couldn't refuse. In a similar fashion, representing my earliest clients, I would lay out, with clarity, the legal and business-world perils of failing to pay a due bill. My client might get his money over a somewhat longer term than originally agreed to. He might get slightly less money than owed. But cash would flow, and the debt would be settled.

Fortunately, my career soon began to morph from sophisticated debt collection to a different sort of adjustment, helping my client firms untangle their own webs of indebtedness, revenue shortfall, and denial. My arrival on the scene signaled the day of reckoning—sorting genuine assets from merely imagined assets, distinguishing cash flow from stale and uncollectable debt, identifying company segments that were losers but perhaps could be turned around by imposing realistic budgets. In other words, I reacquainted a business's operations and balance sheet with reality. It was an interesting professional evolution. I am proud that at first I was one of the very few out there doing such work. Consequently there was no name for it. Eventually phrases like "crisis manager" and "turnaround management" were coined, and entities like the

Turnaround Management Association came into being. Until that time I needed to describe my business in *some* way, which is why fewer than 20 years ago our letterhead and business cards still identified us as: "McTevia & Associates, Management and Adjustment Consultants."

Almost from the beginning I wound up repairing many clients' personal balance sheets as well as their companies'. This was true even though America's personal debt deluge was then a trickle compared to what it would soon enough become. When someone lives the good life via entrepreneurial success, and that good life suddenly goes awry without apparent reason, a personal financial morass and a company's financial morass almost always co-existed in a chicken-and-the-egg relationship. It's what happens when individuals and companies alike don't fully understand that balancing income and outgo is a task that doesn't care about the amount you are balancing, just that it be balanced. "Fatal" is fatal whether a $100,000 entity owes $200,000 or a $10,000,000 entity owes $20,000,000.

The overleveraged companies for whom I did consulting work generally were run by overleveraged chairmen and overleveraged presidents, who generally were CEOs of overleveraged and insolvent families. Insolvency can be rationalized in many ways. Back in the '50s and '60s most such families did not feel insolvent, because they held equity in their very substantial homes. It was taken as a matter of faith and as a matter of fact that the value of a home would forever rise. Both that faith and that "fact" took a beating in the economic crisis that descended on America beginning in 2008. But do keep in mind my remark about the "loosening" of our culture that began somewhere in my early adulthood. When I started out in this business, people not only made down payments on homes, they made substantial down payments. And they bought homes whose value had some realistic relationship to their income. Otherwise, the banks would not even consider a mortgage loan. To say that all these things changed in the following decades would be a monumental understatement. Nonetheless, even back in those less loose, more realistic times I had no difficulty finding overleveraged businesses with overleveraged principals, all desperately in need of being dragged back into fiscal reality, if possible.

Runaway debt is like toxic gas. If it can find a seam, it will get through and spread its poison unless you consciously take steps to keep it out. Ownership equity typically became that seam. How could a business owner with substantial equity in his or her home feel anything other than personally wealthy on paper? The correlation of being broke and a lack of cash never converged because of the apparent cushion of wealth provided by drawing on home equity. Is it any wonder a business owner, still without cash, would then feel secure when his business possessed apparent equity in plant, machinery and equipment? A little cash-flow problem at the shop? Use the equity to float a loan. Take that same kind of flimsy self-assurance back to the personal arena, and family finances begin to look exactly like an overleveraged business. A second mortgage here, a little home equity line of credit there. Along come credit cards, and you put a bit of credit on a new Visa because the MasterCard is tapped out. The family sails happily, it thinks, on into the future. Everyone thinks they are *coping*. Both the business and the family in this picture are, sadly, sailing on a ship of fools. As long as the economy generated ever-higher sales volumes annually, the ever-more-indebted business and household could both float along, like a leaf headed for an unseen storm sewer up around the bend.

Decades ago when our debt tsunami was merely rumbling beneath the surface, NACM, the trade group, became a forum for me to develop the framework called creditors' committees. These are wonderful mechanisms, a way to avoid Bankruptcy Court supervision while exploring solutions to serious financial difficulties. I developed a national reputation for what were referred to as "out of court workouts." That was on the business side of the ledger. Quite naturally, as you might now expect, I soon was using the same mechanism to help owners of troubled companies resolve family financial difficulties. I still use this approach. I don't foresee any end to the need. Good people fall into debt addiction, just as good people become alcoholics. My own observation is that debt is more alluring and more addictive than booze.

My approach might be compared, in fact, to Alcoholics Anonymous or other 12-step programs. There are major differences. But the client admitting the problem is where AA and I both begin a quest to end destructive behavior. The family must *together*—including all kids old enough to understand—do its own debt-centered version of an AA meeting. Good old Dad must stand up and say: "My name is Bill and I am a debt-a-holic." The wife must be clear: "My name is Mary and I am a shop-a-holic" The kids need to chime in and show, in their own way: "I don't know what kind of a holic I am, but I sure like to spend money and I don't even know where it comes from." Whatever script or outline one uses, it is all about admitting a problem, recognizing that each member of the family must share in the solution, and making full commitment to the effort.

The first time I took this approach it seemed natural, and it simply happened. It began at a dinner meeting where the owner and his wife sat down with me to discuss the problem and their options privately. I trained them to chair family meetings. I told them what to say and I did give them a script. The rest was up to them. There is no better example of getting the family's attention and support than Mom and Dad presenting a united front and telling it like it is.

Over the years I've engineered scores of less structured family financial turnarounds. But I've also used the full-bore and scripted approach scores of times. At a number of client companies, brothers, fathers, uncles and cousins all worked for the same firm and relied on it for their income. Those cases generated group meetings of six to 24 people, expanding to families of 25 to 75 people depending on the company's age and success. Insolvent dynasties are all sadly instructive, and some are intensely tragic. What made some people in the Great Depression jump from windows of tall buildings? How can a financial problem lead a person to take his own life? I don't know, but in my career I encountered six people who committed suicide rather than live past that inevitable day of fiscal reckoning. You read similar stories in the news media, even the occasional mass murder of a family by a parent who cannot see a way out of our national addiction, debt.

I have, though, watched a remarkable percentage of "destroyed" individuals emerge in good shape from the collapse of their financial good life. Identifying reality and meeting it face to face usually has a positive effect on any aspect of human life. All the families I have worked with, all the adults and all the kids, learned firsthand that solving a serious financial problem starts by dealing honestly with "stuff." Stuff is something we all have. The American way is to acquire as much stuff, every day, as possible. We have enough wealth to acquire stuff at a rate most of the world cannot imagine. True, modern media have led much of the world to covet stuff (see Iceland) just like Americans. Credit allows us to acquire still more stuff. UPS and FedEx will bring stuff to your door every day just for the asking. Our collections of stuff grow and seem to have lives of their own. The thing is, no one except those in deepest poverty needs all of this stuff to live. Few even need most of their stuff. That is why stuff is the beginning of solving most individual and family financial problems. In many families the quest for stuff is not just the prime symptom of "living beyond our means," but its sole cause. Many Americans con themselves into identifying themselves by their stuff, and believing all that stuff is necessary to any satisfactory way of life. Getting rid of it, for many, means failure. That is the opposite of truth. Success in solving this problem is all about getting rid of stuff. When your income suddenly plummets, that is the first step toward fiscal health and mental sanity.

Dealing with the owner of a troubled business often means dealing with an individual who has *incredible* amounts of unneeded stuff. We really can exist with one home, for example, and do not need the three "Cs" (cabins, condos and cottages). Many Americans—most of them employees, not employers—have more than one home. Many more have time shares and spend money they do not have traveling to properties they do not own, furnishing them with purchases they cannot afford. An analysis of these assets is the first step. Usually there is some equity. Even if what is owed on the properties adds up to no more than what they are worth, getting rid of them has an almost immediate impact on cash flow. Getting rid of them and ending up with some cash is even better because the cash can be used to buy time.

Time is the most critical component of financial problem-solving. With time—as Dr. M. Scott Peck related with great clarity in his phenomenally successful *The Road Less Traveled*—most problems can be solved. Do I believe this? Absolutely. I have proven this repeatedly over the years. Most families dig their way into financial holes over time. So, short of hitting the lottery, why would anyone imagine being able to dig back out overnight? The cash generated from getting rid of a second home or cottage or cabin or condo builds a cushion of time in which to restructure.

For most of the middle class, let alone once-successful business owners, there is lots more "stuff" to be addressed. Toys such as boats, personal watercraft, snowmobiles, ATVs, motorcycles, tractors, trailers, and campers come to mind. Those are examples of expensive toys that, while they may yield some equity, are probably also draining cash flow because they are, of course, not yet paid for and because they need to be fueled and maintained and stored and insured. And there is other stuff—a gun collection or a coin collection, for example—that might not be demanding a check be written each month, but has some value if liquidated. On and on, multiplied by each family member. You get the idea. Get rid of this stuff. That's what eBay is for. You probably will not get millions from selling such stuff, but you will generate funds to buy more precious time. You won't be spending money putting gas in these toys. You won't be making payments on them. These measures are both easy and difficult, which might be said about achieving fiscal sanity at any level in any arena.

I just wrote, in a few paragraphs, a simple and guaranteed blueprint toward peace of mind for an individual or family. There is nothing easy about enduring the pain in losing toys and a lifestyle you have become accustomed to, and the pain of going cold turkey on an addiction. But the moment you start following that simple blueprint you are already making headway. Some meaningful weight is being lifted off a debtor family's aching back. *Sometimes there really is such a thing as pain that feels good.* So don't take my guarantee of pain as a sort of floor-to-ceiling doom and gloom. It's just the opposite. We are talking about creating a genuine light at the end of a very dark tunnel.

That's the picture for an individual or a family living in the future. In the complex arena of an entire culture and its government, the problem becomes infinitely more difficult. I believe the blueprint is every bit as simple. But how much diesel power will it take to push the biggest and most powerful runaway freight train in the world back up the mountain it is barreling down? It's already too late to prevent a coast-to-coast epidemic of pain. But can we avert the worst possible outcome? The short answer would be that my professional experience and my commitment to fiscal realism suggest unbelievably good news... and profoundly bad news.

The unbelievably good news, in my view, is that, yes, we still have for the moment the world's largest economy, and if everyone in the runaway freight's cab treated our economic resources with a little respect and fiscal realism we could...well, *survive* the crisis. Given what I see on this nation's balance sheet, I think survival—pain and all—really would be good news. And I do believe if we made a serious effort, right now, we could achieve it. Now for the profoundly bad news. I don't believe America's leaders will summon the courage to put the country back in contact with fiscal reality. I think they will drag us forward to a day of reckoning that very few right now are willing to foresee. That's what this book is about.

Before scoffing too loudly at that, don't forget that Bernie Madoff's clients included some of the most talented, brightest people in America. They *had* to know they were buying into an impossibly good (read "phony") deal. They might not have fully realized that Bernie Madoff, thanks to them, was living more deeply into the future than anyone else on the planet—but with their help, he did. If people whose talents had earned them net worths measured in many millions of dollars were willing to write checks to Madoff, then it doesn't take much for a politician to woo an average citizen by promising the moon. Teddy Roosevelt, and then Winston Churchill, eloquently promised nothing but "blood, sweat, toil, and tears." But no one noticed Roosevelt's speech, and when Churchill repeated the slogan it was in the face of a threat no one could ignore. Preaching the need for fiscal blood, sweat, toil, and tears in a U.S. electoral race is another story. Such a common-sense and absolutely vital message would lose in a landslide to any politician of either party making less painful promises based on nothing more than the ability of the good old U.S.A. to print more money, spit it out, and borrow it back. Don't forget, clever as Bernie Madoff was, he couldn't print money.

You may have noticed that I am angry about all

this. I'm in the later laps of a life's run that has been very good to me. I love this country. I love my family. I am smart enough to know it is impossible to foresee how technology and nature and demographics will impact what American life looks like at the turn of the *next* century. But I absolutely know the ultimate impact of unsustainable, toxic levels of debt. I can't paint that impact in laser-sharp detail, of course, when it comes to an enterprise as large and complex as the United States of America. I can't say, for example, that a U.S. Treasury default would result in the Chinese owning and operating the Grand Canyon as a theme park. Speculating on the specifics of a default is a fascinating mind game, however, and we'll play a little of that later on. I don't really think, by the way, that China could, or would want to, wind up operating the tourist helicopter franchise at God's Big Dig in Arizona. That's good. On the other hand, I foresee *highly* possible outcomes that are much worse. That's bad.

3

Frustration 101

*Facts which at first seem improbable will,
even on scant explanation, drop the cloak
which has hidden them and stand forth in
naked and simple beauty.*
—Galileo.

Why is there air?
—Bill Cosby.

Writing this book took longer than it should have. In 2009 nearly every day's economic headlines produced a new bouncing ball, a new shell game, a new jaw-dropping negative statistic. It became tempting to research each new twist so as to discuss it in detail...or to sit back and wait for some dust to settle for fear of winding up with a manuscript hopelessly overtaken by events. I finally realized that almost every such news story—past, present, and future...from Wall Street or Washington or around the world—amounts to a red herring. The things I am saying in this book, the parts that really matter, are essentially the same message I tried to convey in

1992 with *Bankrupt.* Like gravity stopping us from drifting into space or the sun coming up in the east, the core of my message is never going to change and is never going to lose its relevance.

Even if mankind unleashed a fusillade of nuclear warheads, odds are strong any surviving historian would find it to be a crime of military insanity preceded by crime of fiscal insanity. Economic disaster as prelude to war has a certain familiarity to it. In the unpredictable chaos of a financial disaster unlike anything seen since before the Hiroshima bomb, no one knows who might push what button. Forecasting a fiery, ironic end to humanity's future as a result of humans trying to live in the future is *not* my message. I mention a nuclear scenario only because one does wonder what kind of wakeup call it will take before enough people seriously care about the ultimate consequences of crippling, unsustainable debt. I'd like to think something less than global thermonuclear warfare would do the trick, but I am not certain that is true.

Events of late 2008 and early 2009, for instance, gave us a wakeup call loud enough to summon the comatose, if not the dead. An exotic chunk of toxic debt, hidden from view like an alcoholic stashes bottles around the house, sent shock waves bubbling up for all to feel and see. We called this debt event's ripple effects a "financial crisis," which it certainly was. You could say we have averted the worst for the moment, which is true. But you also could say we, like Alice, have entered the rabbit hole but haven't yet reached the spot where Alice topples straight down to her famous adventures. What lies ahead for us is yet another, much larger debt event—possibly even, to use terminology from nuclear energy lore, the "China syndrome"...a meltdown capable of burning through the entire world economy as easily as coring a rotten apple.

What bubbled to the surface in 2008 was what everyone called "the subprime mortgage crisis." It marks the approximate point where I began to think about writing this book. I had no 20/20 vision of the book's content and shape. I confess that frustration and anger and "I told you so" were in my first thoughts. But it's also true that as months passed I thought of the project as nothing more than a manuscript to be written exclusively for my children and their children. It would be Grandpa's "legacy book," an apology for several generations of fiscal insanity from which they and *their* children will have to dig out. One always thinks in the back of one's mind that a manuscript *might* be bound between real covers and offered commercially as something others might want to read. And the frustration and anger kept expanding the part of my mind that hopes this message will reach as many readers as possible beyond family and friends. That is not about me. It's about the message. If others find ways to make the truths expressed here take root, I'll be happy. I don't own these ideas. They are worth their weight in gold, but they are in the public domain. If only the public cared.

During 2009 I made several running starts at producing a manuscript while pursuing my busy day job and, like everyone else, gawking at the economic carnage littered along the road. Gradually I decided I *would* try to reach an audience beyond family and friends. I decided this made sense for two reasons. First, I realized that getting plugged into each day's news story, each new proposed political solution, and each new fork in Alice's rabbit tunnel was not vital to this book. Second, I became awestruck that although more and more highly respected officials and analysts are warning about the nation's perilous balance sheet, our people and our media and our leaders refuse to accept the fact that runaway unrealistic debt and still more deficit spending lie at the root of our crisis. Words cannot express my sheer awe at that fact. We are becoming, almost to the decimal point, Iceland times one thousand.

Probably I shouldn't be awestruck. The continuum I described in *Bankrupt* remains unbroken, from the child who spends his allowance before he has it—and then pledges many future allowances to buy something he doesn't need and will wear out long before it is paid for—to policymakers and politicians willing to roll the dice and make wagers backed by trillions of their unborn descendants' dollars. I am no Nobel economics laureate. I am not even an economist. I didn't even attend college. But any Nobel economics laureate who thinks my bottom-line message adds up to nonsense ought to climb down from his tower and walk some of the same ground I've been walking for a very long time.

Most people, even politicians, are wise enough when discussing wars and potential wars to consult those who have been up close to watch the most careful battle plans disintegrate, and to see good people reduced to body parts as a result. It is good to keep a few people in the war room who understand both the people *and* the strategic concepts being pushed around on a map...who tap into indelible real-time experience when drawing future consequences in their mind's-eyes. So it goes with fiscal reality. I do believe experience on the front lines counts for something.

It was, in fact, just before enjoying Christmas 2009 with my family—desperately aware that so many families would not be enjoying this holiday's moments in their accustomed manner—that I took this authoring process out of idle, put it in gear, and stopped trying to fit the narrative into perfect synch with current events. I quit worrying about anyone deriding this effort by saying: "You know, Jim McTevia is not an economist and his new book peddles the same message as his last one!" Damned right it does. Why not? The same train wreck I wrote about in *Bankrupt* is waiting up around a bend, except it's an ever-bigger train wreck. So I'm going to wave that red flag again. I'll try to do a better job. Maybe the second time will be a charm. Maybe events will have stirred at least enough interest to attract some readers.

The pre-Christmas moment that got this book into focus was no epiphany, not even your garden variety new experience. It was something I have done hundreds of times. Let's say at least 200 times. Doesn't sound like a lot? I'm guessing that's 200 times more than any Nobel laureate, or any TV talking head, or any politician holding a wet finger to the wind (and a stethoscope to his voter base). Here's another round number—100, that being the average number of people I have looked in the eye and delivered devastating news on each of those occasions. That would be at least 20,000 people whom I personally have told, essentially: "Your life is in the toilet, and there is nothing I can do about it." The pollsters make headlines about attitudes on war and peace and politics by getting on the phone and asking a few hundred people some hypothetical questions. My cumulative and still-growing sample is much larger, in person, and most definitely not hypothetical. Here is the way it works.

Three weeks before Christmas 2009 I stood before the employees of a regional retailer that had prospered for 65 years. During all that time the company paid its taxes, provided jobs for several generations of workers, offered a quality of goods and services that allowed it to thrive in the marketplace. If each employee represented on average a family of three, then we are talking about enough people, if gathered in one spot, to incorporate a town well larger than the smallest places on a state highway map. It's highly unlikely you know any of these people. All you know is that on this particular workday of mine and theirs, the economic news across the country was that the employment picture was looking somewhat less bleak. Many talking heads, in fact, were into their 10th or 12th cycle of reporting that the Great Recession was easing up nicely, or there was at least some light at the end of the tunnel. The most foolhardy commentators roughly predicted when the bust would go boom.

My own task on that particular day, on the other hand, was to tell these employees that their company was closing shop for good, that they were not being "laid off" but terminated, that they had done good work for a good outfit, that nonetheless considerable pain and adversity lay ahead for almost all of them. I told them that the following week would be their final hours on the clock, and that to pay rent and buy groceries they would have to find another job. I said the only good news I could bring them was that I had seen countless souls endure this very trauma and survive. I wished them well. I did *not* wish them "Merry Christmas."

This sad piece of business is the worst part of my job. It's like attending a funeral where all the mourners believe *they* have died. Speaking to the doomed employees I try to adapt a demeanor that is simultaneously matter-of-fact, assertive, and compassionate—so my audience doesn't feel they are the first people in history upon whom such a fate has befallen, so they don't go into a "there must be some mistake" denial mode, and so they understand no one wants to be doing to them what is being done. My message and my demeanor don't change any facts or put bread on their tables, but my respect for them and compassion for their situation run deeper than the kindest heart among them could imagine. When I must visit a company and make such a presentation in the holiday season it doesn't help that Dickens is

my favorite author. I feel all the more like I have
been cast as Scrooge, except even though I *know* all
about the ghosts of Balance Sheets Past and Balance
Sheets Future, I will never be able to fling open a
window and shout into the street: "Hey, guess what?
It was a mistake! Go back to work! And on the way
home buy a nice big turkey for Tiny Tim!"

To my clients, to their creditors—and to any
Bankruptcy Court if one is involved—these moments
I spend with a firm's employees are a minuscule
part of my job. It's a task that in fact consumes
a minuscule part of my time. My skill in almost
instantaneously recognizing assets and liabilities so
as to head off accidental or intentional deceit is a
key area of expertise I get paid for. Probably more
so is my experience and skill in running interference
and negotiating a doable result for all parties to a
restructuring or liquidation—*none* of whom will
be getting what he wants. Keeping the process out
of court instead of entering the bureaucracy and
inflexibility of legal adjudication would be another
reason my services are engaged. I have skilled
associates in my firm, but I often spend hundreds
of hours personally on one case (one rare winding-
down of a company lasted for three years). Nothing,
though, stays with me like those few minutes standing
before assembled employees who are being told by
events—regardless of what I say—that "listen, pal,
your world just changed, a lot, and it most definitely
is not for the better." I make it a point to show up
and do this personally, largely for reasons stated in
my analogy about war-room planning. These are not

chess pieces on a map, not mere paycheck liabilities. They are people.

At actual funerals, the kind held at funeral homes rather than on a shop floor, the prevailing comment sometimes is that the deceased "lived a full life." At other times the attendees are united in their grief that the deceased was "struck down so soon." Worst of all are those passings where it is said the death, resulting from accident or mayhem or bad behavior, "was all so senseless." So it goes with the death of companies. Businesses do have life cycles. Their natural lifetimes will vary by business type, or by what point in the history of a product or service they entered the marketplace, or by the impact of changing consumer tastes, or by the arrival of game-changing technology, and so on. Regardless of that cycle's timing, perfectly well-managed companies sooner or later mature and ultimately cease to exist. If their natural lifespan doesn't end it all, they will fight on despite being marginalized by any of the circumstances mentioned above until— boom! like an overleveraged Icelander's SUV biting the dust—they succumb in their weakened state to "a bad economy."

There would be no reason to write this book, of course, if I did not—even in good times—preside over so many company and corporate "funerals" that are not natural deaths but fall instead into the "so senseless" category. A company over-leverages into imaginary future profits, raises its head up into the fire zone of risky ventures, reaches further into the future to stay afloat, then takes fatal bullets in its balance sheet. That's a typical demise. Sometimes, though, so many entities in a company's orbit are living so deep into the future that the company at hand winds up as, in military terms, collateral damage.

It used to be said, for example, that "when Detroit sneezes, America catches a cold." That slogan probably predates even Charles Wilson's maxim, voiced in the Eisenhower era, that "what's good for General Motors is good for America." My, how things have changed. Be that as it may, it has been a long time since most people across the country understood the American auto companies' ripple effect on the country's prosperity. Even now, with the Big Three humbled down to the Detroit Three, it nonetheless remains true that what happens in Detroit does *not* stay in Detroit. When things go bad in the auto industry, it affects the economy of every state in the union. And no one—absolutely no one engaged in a legal enterprise—ever lived as far into the future as the American auto companies.

The dismal economic headlines of 2008 and 2009 were anchored by a pair of bookends sculpted from wildly unrealistic debt. The Wall Street side featured putting gullible citizens into homes they couldn't afford (literally living in the future) on terms lenders couldn't afford. The Heartland manufacturing side (or what remains of it) featured outlandishly indebted carmakers (fiscal promises to retirees are real obligations until bankruptcy time—something to remember when pondering Washington's Ponzi scheme). Books already have been written about the government bailouts of General Motors and Chrysler, and the self-bailout of Ford (as good a term as any to describe a company that wisely foresaw impending disaster, and strategically exercised its access to secured debt before circumstance could yank that resource away). More such books will be written. It's an enormously complex thing. That said, what could be simpler and more disastrous than having more retirees than employees, and promising those retirees greater benefits than could be sustained anywhere but in the shared dreams of management and labor? Can there be a more egregious example of living in the future? Do you see anything in that automaker workforce equation—which everyone seems to agree was doomed—that parallels America's "entitlements problem"? Of course you do. It is, in fact, déjà vu, except with far more zeroes in the numbers.

Watching the very large chain of industries surrounding GM, Ford, and Chrysler (larger in fact than the Detroit Three themselves) is like watching one of those guys in a video clip who stacks enough dominoes to fill a convention hall, then tips one and triggers a stupendous flurry of pieces cascading in every direction. Many of these satellite companies were well run. All, for an entire generation, have been forced by the Detroit Three to run many times more efficiently than the Detroit Three themselves. My firm, and others, have been kept busy by these falling dominoes—be they parts suppliers or die makers or suppliers to the suppliers. Yes, any good company is supposed to maintain reserves to endure hard times. But if your company's entire orbit has been poisoned by your principal customers' living in the future, then you are, at best, in trouble. At worst, you're dead.

Such was the case even with that retailer whose employees I faced three weeks before Christmas. So far as I know, the company did not sell a single product directly to the Detroit automakers. But all of this stricken company's customers depended, directly or indirectly, on the health of the American car companies. So the retailer's demise should not have come as a shock. On the other hand, one does not step up before those employees and say, as if the logic of it is somehow comforting: "You should not be surprised by what I am about to say."

But after speaking to these employees, I did not leave work that night pondering how to write about General Motors or parts suppliers or the miserable state of Michigan's economy. Nor, down in the trenches with those suddenly redundant workers, had I seen anything new to write about. I know firsthand the proximate cause for companies (or their creditors or a court), finally, to pick up the phone and ask for my services. What crystallized in my mind that night in December 2009 was a determination to go back to that most basic truth, get this book done, and focus on conveying my steadfast belief that unless our federal government starts living its fiscal life in the present rather than the future, the United States will have no future. Not any future where any of our descendants would rather live than, say, Iceland, where at least geothermal heating is abundant.

The Prologue told you what happened in 1993 when I had the audacity to venture these truths in *Bankrupt*, and took that message to our elected leaders in Washington. It was quite a lonely message at the time. I was not a lone voice in the wilderness. It was more like being in a barbershop quartet competing with a 200-voice choir, accompanied by a pipe organ. On the surface, things have changed quite a bit during those 17 years. One can read, and hear, people far more famous, visible, or academically honored than myself who lately are standing up in public and allowing that it is probably not a good idea to hang the nation's future on trillions of dollars of new debt spent toward uncertain ends. We shouldn't do this at any time, they and I say, much less while we have endless and growing billions in other unfunded obligations. Trouble is, it seems most economists and politicians and pundits and the public itself still live in the future, enjoy living there, and see nothing but good days ahead if we would just bear down and get even more insolvent as quickly as possible.

I worried aloud in *Bankrupt* that unrealistic debt would bring down our republic. I am not only not an economist, I'm not a historian, so in *Bankrupt* I could only assume that living in the future had brought down past empires. So I was delighted toward the end of 2009 to see a Newsweek cover story in which Niall Ferguson expressed the same worry. All of Europe's failed empires, Ferguson wrote, were in fact brought down by debt. Ferguson is a Harvard historian, which is good enough, I would think, to inject this disturbing, compelling fact into public conversation. But even though my work takes me out of the house almost every day, one is not likely to hear anyone at the next table saying in spirited conversation: "Ya know, I think our government's willingness to paper the world with debt is going to bring this country down." As I said, it is a very small step from a child's willingness to spend a year's worth of future allowances to buy some toy today, to a government's willingness to print money, borrow money, spend money without putting it on the books...absolutely anything that will not keep the wolf away from the door, but will push the wolf into the future. Pity the future. It will, soon enough, be the present. Hello, wolf. Bigger wolf.

Nor am I an author by profession. But I am finally so frustrated by our society's and our government's endlessly voracious appetite for raping future generations' prosperity, and by our leaders' refusal even to regard that as a problem, that my vision for this book has changed dramatically. The peril of ignoring the old *Bankrupt* message has soared along with Washington's mountain of debt. I am so skeptical of this society being put on course that I honestly expect the United States, which has never gone into default, will endure some parallel kind of fiscal event, will endure some equivalency of restructuring, will hit some kind of wall—splat! I do not pretend to envision exactly what form this cataclysm will take, but I will not be surprised if it involves more pain than anything seen between the two coasts since the Civil War.

That's an audacious prediction, for sure. But there

it is. With the lessons of my professional experiences having held true for another two decades since *Bankrupt*, and with the federal government still living in a fiscal fantasyland, I can't foresee it any other way. I hope I'm wrong. I hope, in fact, this book will in some small way help influence events for the better. Along with others who insist we must get back to living in reality and in the present, I am re-issuing my warning: "Sorry, Virginia, there is no Debt Fairy. We must eventually pay up, or down we go."

Each of us will press that truth in our own way, from our own life experiences. My experiences involve balance sheets and their inevitable consequences. Mine is a rare vantage point within the world of debt. But uniquely and most humanly my experiences involve standing before so many employees of so many insolvent companies and telling them it's all over. The United States government is not a mere manufacturing company or a chain of retail stores. But I know this, despite the messes I have been called to help clean up across the last 50 years: Most, even a large percentage of, failed companies are better-run than Washington, D.C. Our federal leaders have more resources to play with than any entity on the planet. They have used those resources to become experts at dancing around the perimeter of insolvency. Those resources, however and contrary to popular belief, are finite. We are nearing the point where someone will have to step before the American people and tell them the party is over.

4

Is There Such a Thing as 'Good Debt'?

Everybody in Vanity Fair must have remarked how well those live who are comfortable and thoroughly in debt; how they deny themselves nothing; how jolly and easy they are in their minds.
— William Makepeace Thackeray, *Vanity Fair.*

Avoiding likewise the accumulation of debt, not only by shunning occasions of expense, but by vigorous exertions in time of peace to discharge the debts which unavoidable wars have occasioned, not ungenerously throwing upon posterity the burden which we ourselves ought to bear.
— George Washington, *Farewell Address.*

T he short answer to the chapter title's question is: "Of course."

By "good debt" I don't mean the banker's sense of the word, as in "collectible debt." We are talking from the borrower's viewpoint about whether debt can be

useful, reasonable, sometimes even vital. Yes, it can.
Describing debt with such noble adjectives is not a
contradiction. My own guess—it's only a guess, but
you get the idea—says as much as 80 percent of all
debt is in fact foolish (emphasizing the root word of
"*fool*ish") or worse. But eliminate that 80 percent (or
70 percent or 60 percent) and we'd still have an ocean
of money owed, and 100 percent of it would be "good
debt." We all know from recent experience that just
a little toxic debt goes a long way. Even a minority
percentage of toxic debt can take everything in sight,
good and bad, down the sewer. So in this book about
the impact of harmful debt, we are taking a little time
out to talk about "good debt," and how to use it. Our
society desperately needs to recognize the difference.
Always keep in mind that "good debt" exists only in
finite amounts. A pile of bad debt, on the other hand,
almost always grows until one lender or another
finally says "no more" and the con game ends.

Taking on debt under certain circumstances can
be the proper thing to do, the right course, sometimes
even the only course. This is true despite the biting
irony quoted above from the 19th Century novel
Vanity Fair (resting "jolly and easy" while buried in
debt—now *that's* satire). And good debt does exist
despite the more literal and straightforward warning
George Washington delivered in his farewell, the
same forum Dwight Eisenhower chose to warn about
a "military-industrial complex." And yes, even the
author of this book—commandeering this soapbox to
warn about the mortal danger of *abusing* debt—fully
understands the useful existence of "good debt."

Confession can sometimes capture attention and help make a point, so let me say that *I* am in debt—even though I am in my 70s, still at the helm of a business. If good fortune continues to smile upon my health, and my country's, I expect to generate an income stream until the day I die. And it is entirely possible I will *still* be in debt—if only until my insurance and assets pay off outstanding bills. Like countless older citizens I am a working debtor whose bills are nothing they can't handle without burdening their survivors. Nothing wrong with that. Nor with many other scenarios in which people, companies, institutions, and even governments take on good and useful debt.

I need to make such things clear in this chapter before going on to land some sincere and what I hope will be hurtful body blows against personal habits, national policies, and an entire culture of unrealistic *abusive* debt. Any reader who ends up regarding me as an old codger who simply can't abide the idea of lending and borrowing is not a careful reader. If you meet such a person on the street, please set him or her straight for me. Let them know Jim McTevia is not opposed to calorie consumption, even though we are—by casual observation and scientific conclusion—an increasingly obese nation. That's a problem that is clogging arteries, costing money, and killing people by the millions. So although I realize we'll all die without calorie intake, I also realize we ought to pay some attention to the type and amount of calories we consume as we fuel our way through life. Not only is a dietary analogy to "debt consumption" apt, but our culture's calorie abuse seems to have marched in near lockstep to our debt addiction. I'll let the historians and the sociologists try to chart and explain that one.

Every day for several decades I have found myself wondering why basic truths—one might say obvious truths—such as the consequences of calorie abuse or debt abuse have been ignored more and more by Americans even as they achieve higher and higher levels of education. It makes no sense. How can smartening up a nation result in dumbing down its behavior? This chapter, which readily concedes that certain amounts and types of debt are acceptable, is a good place to ask that question. The only sane conclusion, it seems to me, is that if somebody is paying good money for all this education (and someone is paying a *lot* for it), then it's time to make some adjustments in the way our money is spent educating our kids. When it comes to financial education, I think I have standing to offer a few words of advice.

For any teachers in the audience who already are rising to object, let me say that yes, I understand the impact of influences kids must confront outside the classroom. Tons of important teaching is done far removed from school. Parents? Of course. Who else is the prime teacher of bad habits? What are good old Mom and Dad teaching tykes in the backseat of the third vehicle in a family with just two driver's licenses as Dad swipes plastic in a fast-food drive-through? Wow! French fries and a hot apple pie on credit while riding in a car with a five-year loan, en route from an unaffordable home to a mall where unnecessary purchases will be charged—not to be paid for on the next billing cycle, but to accrue interest...along with previous charges, as well as interest on the three car loans, the mortgage interest (which adds up to 90 percent of the monthly "house payment"), and interest on—wait, can this be right?—*last summer's vacation, including a number of bad meals*! Plus interest on various other impulsive or even whimsical purchases. A substantial village in a Third World country could live on the interest charges paid by a typical American suburbanite. So much for parents as financial role models.

And yes, I understand that we live in a media age of mind-boggling scope. The internet, cable TV, personal communication devices that amount to instantaneous, ubiquitous peer pressure (as well as a conduit for influences far removed from a youngster's peer group)...all these, and new inventions I don't yet know about, exert enormous power upon the behavior of educated adults, let alone the kids we send off to school. Broadcast media often seem like a 19th Century medicine show, peddling wares alleged to enhance sexual pleasure or cure diseases many viewers have never heard of. Once cured, the contemporary couch potato might wish to follow up on offers of learning how to get rich by borrowing money to buy gold coins, or leveraging ownership of a few dozen HUD homes. Nowhere does one find commercials designed to help viewers, young or old, live within their means.

That's what you are up against, teachers and

principals and superintendents and school boards. Sorry about that. The fact that your task is so enormous only leads me to ask why more resources aren't devoted to teaching fiscal sanity. Our young people are being channeled into an adulthood that accepts insolvency as a way of life. That is not acceptable, or even close. Not for these individuals, and not for our society. What you are hearing from me is not some simplistic obsession with tidy bookkeeping. We *need* to be producing a nation of fiscally literate adults. That is an educational imperative. That is a universal requirement for individual survival, and for group survival. It applies to future novelists, painters, engineers, astronomers, filmmakers, historians, bricklayers, mail carriers, truck drivers, teachers, and—talk about a profession exhibiting this need— politicians. Any insolvent human being will be an unhappy human being, and probably a miserable human being. Except of course in that delusional place described in *Vanity Fair*, where debt-ridden living-in-the-future types have no idea how hard they are about to fall. Fiscally illiterate people are not people you want running the company that employs you, or handling the books at, say, the community theater or service club that consumes much of your free time. Financially illiterate individuals, if elected to public office, drive governments into insolvency, unable to deal with crisis.

Financial literacy clearly impacts all aspects of your family's daily life, at home or in the world at large. Which takes us back to the educational system. Teaching fiscal truths in the schools is our last line of defense. The news media can, and will, take a 10-year-old who has never set foot in a classroom and teach him or her hand/eye coordination, lyrics (and dance moves) to every song that's hot, how to go find a sound-bite answer to any trivia question, and how to step in front of a camera and behave just like a 30-year-old news anchor or reality show contestant. But nowhere—*nowhere*—is this media-age kid going to learn that the next page of his real life cannot be written with a charge card.

I am not an educator. I know nothing about the latest teaching resources or methods. No matter. What is failing our children and our society in school-based fiscal education mirrors our entire society's loss of contact with fiscal reality. That is, almost no one in the educational establishment appears to care about, understand, or focus on the problem. In that case, educators—meaning us, because the schools work for us, on our dime—are making a huge mistake. This failure extends from the ghettoes to our most affluent communities. Time now for someone to focus on the problem, put it at the top of the priority list, define a curriculum, and implement it. Professional educators can design the methods and can budget the resources. But I can easily tell you when this newest "school subject" needs to be taught (from the earliest grades to the end of high school), and what basic content our young people must learn.

We need to send high-school graduates off into chronological and legal adulthood understanding that, like power tools and heavy equipment, one's approach to finances can build one's life mansion or tear it down—and can shelter you in comfort or drench you in misery. The concept of living within one's means is something that needs to be stressed throughout grade school. If I am not an educator, how do I know this can be done in grade school? Easy. Because it used to be done at that age via nickel-and-dime allowances for household chores, with snow shoveling and baby-sitting jobs, with newspaper routes. A connection was made between work and income, between sweat and sweets, and between income level and spending level. This is not, as they say, rocket science, but it is more important. And yet here we are in an era where, for all I know, actual rocket science is being taught in grade school, to kids who meanwhile are well on the way to having no sense of how to live within their means.

"But don't you see," I hear the educators say, "it's *the parents*—and everyone else on the outside—who have abandoned this good fight?" Yes. Of course. And as I said, I am sorry. But you try to teach reading even to children of parents who don't read. Teaching financial literacy ought to be even easier. There's no triage to be done. Almost every youngster who comes to you will be financially illiterate. Feel free to teach the subject to every student in every classroom.

I am not sure how far down into grade school the use of credit cards has reached, or will ever reach. I like to think retailers will always say no to a 3'6" tot handing a piece of plastic upward to pay for the latest video game. But then there is the internet, where restrictions on any kind of activity are likely to be hacked by some fifth-grader who is capable of breaking into the Pentagon's computer system. So at some appropriate grade (sixth? seventh?) it is time to explain plastic, explain that swiping that magic card (or typing a very long number into a web site) constitutes a future obligation which, if not met—or even if met—can spike the personal misery index in a big way. Someone has to get through to these kids the fact that good people, including parents, find themselves in trouble by using credit to live beyond their means.

My guess is that the previous paragraph points to the hardest part of this entire matter of fiscally educating all our children. That is, figuring out which more advanced parts of the simple "live within your means" concept can be introduced at what age. Professional educators could have such details ready for next semester if the schools decided to go for it, as they should. What I hope to be the central message of this book, for example, is the inevitable linkage of personal finance to the finance of commerce to the finance of important institutions to the finance of government. That theme needs to be a natural progression in the schools' teaching of fiscal literacy. Toward the close of a K-12 financial education, it should be a natural step to be examining government budgets and balance sheets.

The individual *does* make a difference. And guess what—a financially educated young person will finally make the connection, will become a proactive stakeholder in the electoral process. He or she will, in other words, go out and vote as an informed citizen. Isn't that, and hasn't it always been, a fundamental goal of American public education?

What about teaching the "power tools and sharp-edged tools" part of fiscal education? Well, my friends, we are back to this chapter's central question, to my ungrudging agreement that a certain amount of debt, at a certain time, for a certain reason can be proper and justified. This, too, is a high-school topic, perhaps for juniors and seniors only. In any case, we are not teaching abstinence in this financial curriculum. Just as I would hope our schools could convey some real-life-learning on the obesity front, a financial literacy curriculum must aim for—by graduation time—an ability to consume intelligently. Calories and fiscal obligations alike. Meld phys ed on the calorie front and a little work-for-pay experience (and fiscal classwork) on the financial side and you'd almost have a holistic "fitness and finance" curriculum. But I digress. And I do realize that the education professionals really do have to determine the "when" of it all, among other things.

There will be some disagreement in describing details of "good debt" at the personal financial level. Many academics and others invited to submit parameters and definitions would no doubt disagree with me on specifics. I do have unusual standing in that area, however, and I think some might be surprised how many others with experience in my field would agree 100 percent with the way I would sort personal debt into "good" and "bad" bins. Good debt, unfortunately, is often more a necessary thing than a positive thing. A well-led, vigorous discussion of these items—and others—would make for a lively class session...and writing assignment.

Good Debt

■ Buying a home while paying at least 20 percent down, with monthly payments no greater than one week's income.

> Footnote #1: The recent crisis driven by abusive debt of countless types sure didn't do property owners any good.
> Footnote #2: Anyone who followed the above rule is doing way better than anyone who did not.

■ Borrowing in the face of a medical crisis, with no or insufficient insurance coverage. Avoiding care and dying as a result is not a good counter-option. Such borrowing might lead to a bankruptcy. Being alive in bankruptcy is much better than being dead and solvent.

■ You have lost your job but another is on the way. You need to tread water. You are not deluding yourself about that next job, and it will not take so long to arrive that you need to downsize your life immediately. Stay in your current dwelling, eliminate frivolous spending, devote yourself to making that next income source arrive as soon as possible.

■ Purchase or lease of a primary vehicle, use of which includes transportation to work, paying 20 percent down with monthly cost no greater than half a week's paycheck. It can be done. Used to be the norm, in fact. As for a second or third vehicle for a spouse or offspring who does not work— maybe. Getting a low-priced, reliable used car could be an honest expenditure if the rest of your family's balance sheet leaves room.

Bad Debt

- Buying a second home on credit. No way. Being buried under a mortgage can be a defensible thing, under circumstances outlined above. Being buried under two mortgages is insane.

- Purchase of toys—boats, snowmobiles, ATVs, etc. No way. Life gives us many challenging decisions about using credit for important and useful needs. If you have enough income to generate credit for things you don't need, you have enough income to get rid of some existing debt—and maybe negotiate more favorable terms. All of which will get you in a position to buy that toy cash and carry.

- Parents nearing retirement, borrowing to finance children's higher education. Not acceptable. Among other reasons, there is no reason to think that education will guarantee the kids being able to support now-broke parents in their retirement.

- Vacations. You may believe this one makes Jim McTevia the Grinch who stole July. Does anyone not charge vacations unless they are rich? Yes. Anyone not living in the future. Do you really want to spend the next year working to pay for a vacation you already took?

- Using juggled charge cards to sustain a lifestyle while barely paying more than the minimum payment (in many cases paying hardly anything beyond interest). This is suicide or a death sentence, depending which metaphor you prefer.

An Example of Good Business Borrowing

■ Any business in transition, with good and honest short-term and longer-term cash-flow projections showing losses and then profits after six months or even a year. Ford Motor Co.'s "self-bailout," borrowing against all its assets so it would have cash to support losses while restructuring, made supremely good business sense. Foreseeing impending disaster, Ford strategically exercised its access to secured debt before circumstance could yank that resource away. It was a classic move that bought time for restructuring amid one of the car industry's darkest moments.

Examples of Bad Government Debt

■ Using Chinese money—well, American dollars borrowed back from the Chinese—to finance trips to space, or pork barrel projects, or fascinating pieces of scientific research of no discernible relevance to ordinary people.

■ Going to war and sending the bill to your grandchildren and great-grandchildren. This is cosmic charge-card juggling on the saddest possible scale. This is something our very first president— the general who led our successful revolution— deplored a couple centuries before the charge card was invented.

Perhaps some of the above items will be viewed as beyond K-12 comprehension or suitability. Perhaps some will be deemed too ideological. I would disagree in both cases. Our youngsters must learn to make a realistic connection between income and outgo, at the personal level and at every other level. A high-school student should graduate, for example, with genuine understanding of who paid for his September-to-June learning experiences and extracurricular activities, how much was paid, and how.

Could there be any more serious educational need at this moment in our society? We don't need a Sputnik to propel a space race. We don't need a generation of malnourished military draftees to generate a school lunch program for the poor. We don't need any more cultural blips such as "L.A. Law" spiking enrollment in our law schools. Of course we need kids who can read better, and who can do enough math to attend engineering school. Looking around at American popular culture I even wish we were producing new generations with greater appreciation for my favorite author, Charles Dickens. But our escalating financial ignorance is leading us toward the world's first major national bankruptcy since the great European empires got cooked in their own cauldrons of debt. If that happens, school boards won't be worrying about how to fund a new performing arts center, or Olympic pool, or how to improve teacher compensation.

I can hear educators shouting, "He's just another guy who wants us to be remedial teachers!" Yes. Absolutely. But I never said it was your fault. We have a much better chance of success imparting these basic and vital fiscal truths in our schools than we do among our population of credit-maxed adults. We need to see kids emerging from school saying: "Why would anyone ask if there is such a thing as 'good debt'? Of course there is." But we need them also to understand, by their knowledge of debt abuse's perils, exactly what "good debt" is. Achieving that happy day is, as I said, an imperative.

We are living so far into an imaginary future and spending so many imaginary dollars that I am not at all sure we have time to prepare a new generation of fiscally sane Americans to set their nation on a sustainable course. The final chapters of this book will explore my thoughts about that. Here let's just say that we are flirting with a debt-driven fiscal event of such destructive impact that no one then would need to argue forcefully for an emergency financial curriculum in our schools. It would be like rushing, at the height of the Great Depression, to offer a class revealing that hard times are possible.

That's the pessimistic side. I do try to voice an optimistic alternative. The only one I can see is the old space program paradigm, which anyone under 40 has been hearing all his life: "If we can put a man on the moon, then we can (fill in the blank)." I suppose it's possible that if we launched a fiscal education program with the intensity we summoned for the space program, we might avert the worst possible disaster. Especially if the effort somehow spilled beyond the schools and jolted a little fiscal sanity into Americans who left high school long ago. Much more to come in these pages regarding prospects for solving our debt disaster.

Meanwhile, for educators, good news: Any recovery, any course correction, from however a difficult spot, will require a long-term assault on fiscal ignorance. That means lots of work for teachers. If we are about to arrive, finally, at a moment when America faces up to the crisis, that will mean our schools are about to take on the most important practical education of our time.

5

Credit Where Credit is Due

*An honest man's word is as good as
his bond.*
—Miguel Cervantes, Don Quixote, Part III.

*Prince Henry: Did I ever call for thee to
pay thy part?*
*Falstaff: No. I'll give thee thy due; thou
has paid all there.*
*Prince Henry: Yea, and elsewhere, so far
as my coin would stretch: and where it
would not, I have used my credit.*
—Shakespeare, King Henry IV, Part I.

I f all the world's a stage, then an endless stream of
scripts and players flows from the world of commerce
and finance, just as from any other walk of life. Whenever
I am cast in a professional role it means the plot has
spiraled downward past all chance of being a comedy.
McTevia & Associates never gets an opportunity to play
for laughs. All our cases are dramas. When the misery
we encounter runs neither broad enough nor deep
enough to qualify as grand tragedy, we nonetheless toil
amid sadness and dread and tears.

Not once in half a century have my services been engaged because things were going well for my new client. That's why many business owners would rather not appear with me in a scene as innocent and benign as "Jim and Bob Do Lunch for No Reason But to Discuss Old Times." Being noticed talking with me over a simple salad, they fear, might mistakenly suggest they have engaged my firm, some "adjustments" are about to be made, and doing business with them might not be a good thing. That's silly, really. Restructurings or liquidations are not ordinarily launched over a cheery meal in a fine eatery. But I fully understand. One easy solution to adjust the misperception, by the way, is to organize a lunch for six or eight. They can't *all* be troubled businesses.

The drama in a restructuring case usually adds up to unremarkable and dull stuff except, of course, for those unfortunate to be playing real-world roles. A bankruptcy can go unnoticed by the world at large despite a cast of hundreds or as many as a thousand or two. Some of these people will be, as they say, "ruined." If the problem runs deep enough to require liquidation, that company's entire cast will need to find new jobs. But without clearly defined heroes or villains onstage, preferably famous ones, a day at our office rarely adds up to a story that will capture much attention from an outside audience.

The view from my front-row seat, however, always has been compelling. Going straight to the financial truth of a company's troubles and resolving the situation in an orderly fashion with all due speed is a fair summary of my job description. I pursue my cases with well-documented objectivity and professionalism. Prospective clients know their companies' products and services far better than I could if I studied them full-time for a year. That's why new clients often do not understand or believe, at first, that after just one hour of analyzing numbers I comprehend their *fiscal situation* and know their options better than they do. I could, yes, tell you a few things about the business of yacht-building or making extruded plastic parts or tool and die making or commercial bakeries. But I could tell you only a *few* such things, and only as a result of having walked the shop floor of those, and many other, enterprises while serving as a financial consultant or court-appointed trustee.

So it's true that I am a numbers guy whose various skills include a good, quick eye for details and what they mean about keeping a troubled business's doors open or closing them. Hardly anyone—maybe no one—has done this work as *long* as I have, and my meter is still running. Perhaps the most important thing I have learned is that despite the incredible range of diversity among clients—the huge and obvious differences between operating a butcher shop or baking bread or making candle sticks— all melt into the same pot when it comes to fatal fiscal problems. A butcher's unsustainable fiscal trajectory looks exactly like a baker's unsustainable fiscal trajectory.

All troubled companies' balance sheets speak the same language and negotiate the same cash-flow pathways. The percentage of revenues eaten up by debt service will determine whether a mom-and-pop furniture store survives or goes bankrupt. The same fiscal dynamic applies to an intercontinental airline with thousands of employees and billions of dollars worth of equipment. It seems obvious to me that the federal government, despite its ability to print money and to borrow cash on every street corner of the world, also can accrue only a finite amount of debt and "spending obligations" before it, too, taps out. My decades of experience as a "numbers guy" in the business world is the standing from which I said this in *Bankrupt* in 1992. Since then it has become easier and easier to find an analyst here and a policy advisor there speaking out about the perils of living in the future. Some even use that phrase. By 2010 one was hearing "unsustainable debt" from the mouths of some politicians, not that Washington, as of this writing, is doing anything meaningful about it.

The managers of our $13,000,000,000,000 (think "tr") national debt somehow remain at least as unresponsive to the obvious disaster they are sailing into as, say, the owner of a debt-buried and doomed 15-employee tool and die shop. Using that same mom-and-pop-sized denial as a reason to ignore something that threatens our entire country's future fuels my anger. It helps explain why I went ahead with another book even though more and more voices have joined in warning about our ticking debt bomb. I hope my vantage point from the bottom line of so many dysfunctional balance sheets gives my warning insight and hands-on credibility. I seek to make a meaningful and I hope compelling addition to the national debate about fiscal sanity. To that end, the next chapter will get to the pressing business of giving our government a thrashing it so well deserves. But first I want to tell you a just little more about the professional experiences that lead me to see things the way I do.

My day-in, day-out experience amid fiscal carnage is akin, I suppose, to a 1950s cancer surgeon. He didn't need an army of researchers following science out the window to know the tar found in his patients' autopsied lungs had fundamental bearing on their demise. Similarly, it means something that virtually all McTevia & Associates clients have called on me for help only after borrowing every dime lenders would lend them to advance into the future. Most could have called me much earlier and emerged in far better shape, which is a serious understatement. To be fair, it did take some very busy professional years for me to master the essential truth I am describing as simple and obvious. So I'll do my best in this chapter to let you observe from my vantage point. My hope is that you will then look out at our nation's fiscal landscape, be appalled, and say—as Pogo said in decrying a different sort of pollution in a poster for Earth Day 1970: "We have met the enemy, and he is us."

The numbers I work with professionally are sign language that tells a business narrative. Each column is a placeholder for genuine (or imagined) assets, liabilities, and cash on hand. Together they offer a window into how far that business is living into the future—its debt and other fiscal obligations, and its ability (for good or bad) to borrow more money or attract more capital. One makes sure the realities match up with the balance-sheet numbers, and one goes from there. That's pretty much all there is to it, if one is required to say it in a sentence or two. But I—or anyone else, in my opinion—would need to be under heavy sedation to avoid being drawn into the stories and people behind each troubled balance sheet.

It's important to understand that my clients over the years, the people driving these numbers, have not only been real people but in the overwhelming majority *good* people. Bad things do happen to good people. Good people shoot themselves in the foot with bad business decisions, or careless business decisions, or by not adequately monitoring someone else's bad business decisions. Most did not even realize the course they were setting for their businesses, themselves, and their loved ones. But all the world *is* a stage, and in my business like any other one encounters good guys, bad guys, and a large number of guys whose hats are neither white nor black but various shades of gray.

In my earliest days, just out of high school and in the most entry-level job description where credit problems are concerned, many of the bad folks I encountered were as often sad or amusing, or both, as they were villainous. Their (and my) minor roles amounted to mere skits—finding the spot where a seriously delinquent "owner" hid that new '55 Crown Victoria when he wasn't driving it, or confronting a small commercial loan customer and "adjusting" his revenue stream to satisfy the bank. I was good at my job even way back then. Many of my training-wheels days were *The Pink Panther* in reverse, with almost everyone *except* Clouseau making wrong turns, tripping over the furniture, and winding up with the punch bowl upside down on his head.

Very quickly, though, I was dealing with bigger fish. Humor became rare. Story lines became sad, then sadder. My job no longer involved a car going back to the bank, or a small cash-flow problem to be tipped in favor of my client. Soon I was operating at the heart of countless cases where clients faced repossession of life itself, or what they had come to define as living. No more toys, no more country club memberships, no more matched pairs of luxury cars, no more shopping vacations for the wife, no more second home in Florida and no more time-share in Aspen. Worst of all and too often, I saw people— my clients or the objects of my clients' attempts to become whole—discover that these material goods and services, all this meaningless and redundant *stuff*, all the prestigious frosting on their upper-middle-class cake...was the very thing that defined them among their circle of alleged friends. Often these were people who had never known any other way of life, because the goose laying the golden eggs had been a creation of Dad or Grand-Dad. The largest number I have seen in a career dominated by much larger nominal numbers was that *six* I mentioned earlier, people who killed themselves rather than carry on in a redefined, downsized existence. This most extreme result of materialism is a very, very sad thing, possibly the saddest possible outcome of the human condition. Those six are not mere placeholders. They are people I will never forget.

Aside from my family, the thing that has given me the greatest comfort in this life has been an aptitude, honed across decades, for helping clients and their own families confront—financially and psychologically—greatly reduced circumstances. Sometimes it goes better than other times, obviously. We are not talking, after all, inconsequential loss. Being able to dine on whatever food you like wherever you like whenever you like *is* quite a different thing from making Friday night at Wendy's your treat of the week. Putting the kids on a bus to perhaps not the best public school in the county rather than boarding them at a private school that produces judges and actors and senators *is* a bit of a switch. Those are extreme examples, to be sure; but I've seen them. My own preference for living life in Column A rather than Column B is one reason I plan to work right up to the day I'm no longer able to do so. Maybe that's one reason I became good at the emotional counseling part of my profession, which is not even in the job description. When I explain to someone that seriously downsizing one's life does not mean the *end* of one's life, far more often than not my client understands I've done well in business but there have been times I also have, as older generations say, had to make do.

Just as I set out to put this chapter together, in fact, I delivered the eulogy for an old friend who became my neighbor when, as a young adult,

I needed to downsize my own family's life. I had entered into a land contract for a house that, as it turns out, we could not afford. I was not yet fully versed in the financial laws of nature. We were forced to give our fine house back to the seller (who was unhappy, of course). My family was even less happy, having lost not only a new home, but also having lost the down payment and having to move into far more modest rental digs. It happened that our new residence, despite its decidedly lesser quality and size, sat across a road from some very expensive lakefront homes. In those days, with babies and doctor bills and a determination not to be a lifelong renter, I worked at my day job, worked at the first paltry stages of a consulting career, and worked at anything else where I could find an hour or two's pay. Hence it was that I began cutting grass and doing other maintenance for a wealthy Detroit industrialist's summer lakeside estate across the street. He allowed our family to use the beach, and our daughter soon became friends with the daughter of the industrialist's neighbor. The neighbor was a great guy and another successful businessman. It was only natural that we eventually became friends with the parents of our daughter's new friend. The father was well-known and highly respected. Despite our dramatically different financial and living circumstances, our friendship became close and enduring. And when I delivered his eulogy, I could not help noting that in extending his friendship he knew—and cared—absolutely nothing about my current financial condition and future prospects except that I would probably be a damned good lawn maintenance guy as long as my legs held out.

So although my teenage years handling coal below decks of Great Lakes freighters paid me more money than my father was making at the time...and although I have for some years made a very decent living in a profession I helped invent...it's also true that I had a couple years' opportunity to be up against it, financially speaking. Not starving-in-the-slums up against it. But if there had been a Wendy's back then, its fare would have looked like a Friday night treat to my family. I have always understood why someone does not want to go backward after reaching a certain level of financial success. I believe I can even understand what it means to lose all your toys and privileges when you have never known a life without them. A little grounding in the real world is a valuable thing in my line of work.

Every once in a while my path has crossed that of a good person who has done a remarkable number of good things in the community for years, then wound up doing something bad enough to cross the line into criminality. The epitome of such a story, in my professional experience, was a man we'll call the Grocer Thief. He got his just reward in the end, and I had a lot to do with the story ending that way. Still, I can't help thinking of his years as a solid citizen and philanthropist. You know about the danger of slippery slopes. In our lifestyles and material aspirations most of us negotiate slippery slopes every day, in ways big or small. For whatever reason, the Grocer Thief suddenly took a header straight down the slippery slope that is greased entirely by greed. It's difficult to imagine a more headlong descent.

The Grocer Thief entered my life when I was called late one Saturday night by a close friend and attorney. He asked me to become receiver of a successful, high-profile grocery chain. Its two owners launched a shareholder spat that had overflowed into a lawsuit, ending up in a very public court battle. That kind of publicity is a bad thing for any company, let alone a company that sells food to consumers. Competition jumps at the opportunity to go after the struggling firm while it is in court, which means the best action is to get the company out of court ASAP. My job as receiver was to operate the company, find funds to pay its bills, and keep it afloat until shareholders could solve their problems and see the matter dismissed from court supervision. That would not be an especially unusual task for my firm and its many experienced associates, so I quickly accepted. Unwittingly I was walking straight into the most blatant gross mismanagement and fiscal irresponsibility I ever have encountered. This was years before Bernie Madoff made the front pages, and we are talking about millions rather than billions. But the mess at hand was driven by greed running every bit as rampant. If Ponzi schemes sometimes dealt in vegetables, this grocery chain's produce department would have been stocked to the ceiling. In fact, the Ponzi schemer was more or less victimizing himself in order to make a killing.

The stores had plenty of experienced employees, many of whom had been with the company more than 30 years. Management ranks were also well experienced. The business had operated at a barely profitable level in a highly competitive arena where margins are low and pennies make the difference in survival. The company, however, had no cash and was struggling to stay alive. It was in court not because of its business problems but because of the shareholder dispute. Each shareholder accused the other of fraud and deception (one turned out to be right), and each insisted on continuing as a part of day-to-day management. My first step was to solve that problem by firing both principals. I did not get holiday cards from either that year.

My staff soon pointed toward the surprising fact that the chain bought almost its entire grocery inventory from a single major supplier, rather than using separate vendors for dairy, meat, produce, etc. It took some digging but we learned that this major supplier was controlled and secretly owned by one of the two battling shareholders. We compared prices and conducted an industry analysis. It became instantly clear why the company had no cash. The major supplier—a shareholder arguing in court that he was a fine and fit steward for this company—was delivering inventory on a COD basis, collecting cash from the cash-strapped company before the products could even be placed on the shelves. His wholesale prices were in some instances two or three times higher than industry averages. The grocery company he was fighting to control was going bankrupt day by day, and he was the reason. Without major intervention the chain would soon be out of business.

We dug in and worked hard, almost literally 24/7, for several months. Unfortunately, we were not able to save the company. We sold several stores to competitors, and closed others. Hundreds of people lost their jobs, creditors lost millions, and—after my firm in its capacity as receiver brought in the FBI and the U.S. attorney's office—the shareholder with his hand in the cookie jar went to jail. This was one restructuring drama that did attract a large audience of outside observers. That happens when you add a criminal prosecution, and a company where scores of thousands of citizens buy their bread and milk, to the mix.

There is a point to this tale that decades ago the tabloids would have called an "amazing true story." The villain was outwardly a good guy, well respected in the industry for many years, a successful operator of his own business, a family man, a political donor, a community supporter, owner of two homes and a large yacht and even a jet plane. But in the end large-caliber greed shot him down in a way that makes no sense at all, unless you have looked inside the dynamic of leveraging and overleveraging and borrowing to the hilt, and past the hilt. When someone wants more of everything, and makes that quest his reason for living, nothing makes sense except finding ways of getting it. The Grocer Thief bought half of a company that was never going to do him any good unless he raped it. So rape he did— the company, its employees, and its suppliers. He insisted on having what he could not afford and was willing to do anything to get it.

Pardon me for seeing a certain continuum here based on my professional experience. The Grocer Thief certainly was a crook committing villainous acts. He committed crimes. But how much different was the Grocer Thief from any person who finds ways of accessing money—in the form of loans that can never be paid back—to continue living in a manner to which he has become accustomed? How much different from someone incurring debt without the remotest possibility of repayment and then, when the clock runs out, walking away from a mortgage and seeking short sales and "haircuts" on other debts? Is that theft? If it doesn't break a law, is there not a greedy line connecting all these behaviors? What of a government promising its citizens things it cannot deliver? Is it a crime that we all fully realize Social Security is going to go bankrupt, but Congress has borrowed Social Security revenues for other purposes? Or even if that were a crime, which it isn't, is it even more *not* a crime because our Congress has promised so much that the program would go bankrupt even if lawmakers hadn't taken the money? Clear-cut answers to questions of criminality are not what's important here. It's that continuum, that connective tissue, that greedy slope that—sadly—has come to define so very much about who we are these days.

I accepted the grocery chain's case the way McTevia & Associates took on the vast majority of cases in the first three decades or so of the firm's existence. Turnaround management, as my line of work finally came to be known, meant exactly that.

A firm would hire us, or its creditors or a court would hire us, to turn a failing company around and send it back into the business arena bruised and leaner but healed and, hopefully, ready to regain competitive traction. The Grocer Thief's remarkable chicanery wasn't known until we uncovered it. As wildly improbable and devastating as his scheme was, we still took our best shot at keeping the company in business. That's what *our* business was all about. Nominally, that's still true. When the opportunity arises, we remain leaders in ability to turn a heavily listing balance sheet upright by scraping off barnacles of debt, tossing misplaced ballast overboard, and putting an operation in sailing trim. But at some point in the last decade and a half I began to notice a fundamental—it's OK if you say "stunning"—change that has great bearing on every topic and subtopic of my message.

First it was a trickle, then a flow, then a current strong enough to erode bedrock attributes that had defined interpersonal business relationships as long as I could remember. In most recent years it has become something akin to a riptide. The very idea of a financial obligation being a meaningful thing is being swept away. When I entered the work force, few things in this society were as damning as to be labeled "bankrupt." People, and businesses, even amid the most adverse fiscal circumstances, pursued every effort to make their creditors as whole as possible. Walking away at the earliest opportunity and expecting to be back in business the next day with a new slate, including new capital, was not standard operating procedure. It was, in fact, rare. Most entrepreneurs regarded "giving a haircut" to banks and creditors as a shameful thing, a subject they hesitated to broach even with someone in my business. I can't draw you an exact timeline of the steps in which that all changed. But it did.

The trend has been as easy to see as if one were, say, a steakhouse waiter who over time began to find customers not tipping, then escalating into quarrels over the dinner check's arithmetic, then finally, in quickly increasing numbers, skipping out the door without paying—all the while seeing nothing wrong with these new behavioral standards. In fact, if "everybody else is doing it" satisfies as a benchmark for behavior, who can quarrel? Skipping out on the check—not for a relatively trivial item such as the finest meal at the finest restaurant in town, but for amounts of money the disappearance of which used to mean prosecution—has become commonplace.

Let me be frank in telling you that honest people still operate businesses that go bankrupt. Bad things still happen to good people. But the percentage of businesses flown straight into the ground by dishonest people has soared, to mix a metaphorical verb. I'm not naïve enough to suggest it once was possible to follow the money down a dark alley and never find anything lurking back there but integrity and honor. I am not suggesting that when I started out in the '50s the unemployment rate among police and prosecutors was 80 percent. The bad guys always have found creative ways of hiding assets. But I have never seen so much of that as I have in recent years. Not long ago, for example, I was liquidating a company that was supposed to have isolated all its physical assets in a fenced-in area. We found, however, charge-card receipts for storage facilities where important assets had been squirreled away in an effort to make creditors as "unwhole" as possible. That kind of behavior has become rampant.

I need to point out that potential clients who come to us looking for less than honorable representation—who walk in the door shopping for the practitioner who will give their creditors the biggest haircut—are not clients we wish to take on. And when they hear my own take on their situations, *they* don't want *us* to represent them. So when I talk about an epidemic of hidden assets and the like I am mainly speaking of scams we uncover as agents for creditors committees, or after being engaged by a bank to see what can be salvaged for both the bank and a troubled client, or—rarely these days—Bankruptcy court. Those are all positions from which I observe toxic balance sheets, a 360-degree view much like a Photographer circling his subject matter. The change is an amazing thing. Instead of helping a business get "turned around" after reaching into a future that has consistently been better than the past, most businesses we deal with have reached so far into the future that they have nothing left to reach into. All we can do is help them into liquidation with a soft landing that is painless as possible. But there *will* be pain.

It is with only a slight hint of satire that I tell you a typical pro-bono hour with a prospective client these days goes something like this, greatly compressed.

Client: McTevia, we want to hire you to save our business.

McTevia: Why? It's losing money like crazy, all the shareholder money is gone, and the business is now bleeding creditors' money.

Client: But if we go out of business, the creditors will lose everything.

McTevia: But that is exactly what is happening to the creditors now.

Client: I need you to talk to the bank and reason with them. They won't lend me any more money.

McTevia: Neither would I.

Client: Then if you won't help us borrow money to save our business, we will find someone who will.

McTevia: Good luck. Start by looking in the Yellow Pages under "Charitable Institutions" because any loan to your business would be a charitable contribution to support your employees, who will soon be out of work.

Client: OK. I'm sorry. I get it now. The free ride with my creditors' money is over. How will I support my family?

McTevia: You won't, not the way they live now. But if everyone downsized and worked, you would survive.

Client: That's not the American way.

McTevia: That, my friend, is the problem.

So in truth, a whole lot of the turnaround management business has become the "softest possible landing liquidation business" or, very often, working on behalf of the creditor(s) seeking to secure an inch or two of solid ground in several feet of quicksand.

Even before this timeline of which I speak, one *always* encountered people or companies willing, amid serious financial difficulty, to ignore obligations, borrow more and more, and stiff their creditors. I need to keep repeating that sort of thing so you don't think I'm merely being nostalgic for a Golden Age that never existed. But the percentage of this behavior increased markedly as the '50s fiscal ethic of Archie and Edith Bunker became old-hat comedy material. The so-called Great Recession that began in 2008, and the Great Uncertainty ongoing as you read this, only made things worse. It's a massive chicken-and-the-egg puzzle, for sure, this matter of what happened to the idea of entering into an obligation with serious intention of fulfilling it. This is not the place for clearing a table and lining up subprime mortgages and credit default swaps and all the rest into a domino string and trying to say who caused the mess. Instead of playing that game, I would merely suggest that how people and companies and institutions and governments relate to debt—both ethically and on a balance sheet—accounts for much that is bad about where we have gotten ourselves, much that is bad about where we seem headed, and much of the answer to the question: "Can we possibly, well, *turn it around?*"

Down here on the fiscal ground where people like myself work, my fellow professionals will tell you that they too have lately observed not just a willingness but a first goal of clients to be something like this:

"I want my creditors to take less money than I owe them, *even if what I owe is secured debt.*" That is a definite "Wow!" along the continuum of fiscal ethics. We are talking not just of promises to pay, but the pledging of assets that were meant to make a loan less risky, therefore maximizing a lender's willingness to lend and the amount of money he was willing to put in the borrower's pocket. When a means is found to stiff that particular lender, it is a heavy hit indeed. Our bad economic times have made this a daily occurrence. Probably more like hourly. That's because collateral—the things pledged so a borrower could live as far as possible into the future—has plunged in value. Which means walking away from it leaves a lender in very bad shape. For instance and in many cases, it has meant being in the hands of the Federal Deposit Insurance Corporation...or in the hands of another lender after a pennies-on-the-dollar merger gave the first lender's shareholders a Marine recruit haircut.

Everyone knows about consequences of the "subprime crisis" that made it possible in Phoenix to buy a six-year-old, five-bedroom house with three baths and an in-ground pool for less than the cost of putting two SUVs and a boat in the garage. It is easy to see what it means to the bank or mortgage company to whom the mortgage-holder sent the keys before walking away. So much for collateral. Not that the bank necessarily wasn't as greedy and fiscally unrealistic as the builder and the homebuyer. (And it is easy to see, at this writing, that much more of this sort of real estate bomb—with untold consequences for the economy at large—lies ahead.) Less apparent to the general public has been the meltdown's effect on other allegedly secured loans in the business world. Take, for example and for starters, an entirely hypothetical piece of real estate in the *temporary* housing market.

Let's say a person bought a luxury hotel for $50 million and a year or two later, amid the economic downturn, was unable—because of his own over-optimistic attempt at living in the future—to keep making his loan payments. His bank eventually had to take back this $50-million albatross even though it won't bring more than $20 million on today's market, assuming one can find a buyer. How does that story end? The bank takes a haircut, for sure. It is meantime entirely possible that on the day a new owner takes over, absolutely nothing about the hotel changes from a guest's point of view. It always was a good hotel. It remains a good hotel. It always had good restaurants. It still does. The room rates are unchanged. Occupancy during the slump had fallen to 50 percent. It remains at 50 percent. The only thing that has changed is that ownership has transferred from someone whose cost of money— his debt service—required 90 percent occupancy to stay afloat, to someone who can make a slim profit at 50 percent.

But real estate is highly visible. Let's go to the world of retailing and manufacturing, a world where I spend most of my time. You have read news stories guessing what percentage of the economy's lost jobs ever will "come back." It's only a guess, but we all know that millions of jobs—especially in manufacturing areas where the exodus to cheap labor abroad has only increased—are gone for good. How deeply into the future do you suppose all the failed machine shops and parts makers and other bread-and-butter manufacturers had reached? That's right. As far as they could. This means they had, in the aggregate, a mountain of debt. And how much on the dollar do you suppose banks and other lenders got for all that manufacturing equipment when there finally was no choice for either bank or businessman but to lock the doors and send everybody home? Right. A pittance.

What I am saying here, and other professionals will affirm, is that fiscal ethics already were sliding down a slippery slope, into the arms of this recession. Talk about a marriage made in heaven. Our economy has become history's largest barber shop. No matter where you turn, someone is getting a haircut. Home "owners" who are gainfully employed at the same income they enjoyed five years ago, but are underwater in the market value of their homes, have no problem walking into the bank and saying "I don't want to pay this much." The bank will look at its options in the current market. The bank can sue (there's a good way to spend money tying up your money). The bank can foreclose (there's a good way to sell a $500,000 house for $200,000). Or the bank can accept the mortgage holder's offer. Quite likely it will be the latter...meaning the guy living at 123 Future Lane either got his house payment cut in half or he walked away from an obligation without penalty. There has been a lot of talk lately about whether this is fiscally ethical behavior on the home owner's part. Hey, give him some slack. He's just a person, not a company or an institution. He is not doing anything illegal. And he now, as a U.S. citizen, owns a piece of General Motors and Chrysler, two cases in which so much hair-cutting happened that it is difficult to clarify whose curls are on the floor. It is fast becoming fact that in this country one need not worry about fulfilling financial obligations because one can always fulfill those obligations for less than what one swore he was obligated to do. (You might need to read that sentence twice, but it's as accurate as it is confusing.)

Let me tell you about two typical prospective clients who came to me recently for help but did not become clients. I am disguising their identities for obvious reasons. Smith and Jones typify numerous prospective clients in that we soon realized we didn't want to represent them, and they soon realized they didn't want to be represented by us. Helping someone to a soft landing is one thing. Helping Balloon Boy's dad land a reality show is something else. There must be reasonable effort to get real, or there is no reality. Not in my book.

Smith and Jones were certified professionals practicing in a partnership. It matters not whether they were accountants, lawyers, surgeons, architects, or interior decorators. Identical financial dynamics can surface in any profession. In my business, referrals usually come from other professionals, or from lenders seeking to save as much as possible from a bad commercial loan. In this case, Smith and Jones knocked on the door after a bank gave them the names of several people, myself included, with expertise in bailing out troubled businesses. The gratis face-to-face initial session McTevia & Associates offers its prospective clients is an opportunity to size up the troubled business (and of course its principals) to see if the case would be a good fit. That means, for example, assessing our ability to help the person(s) at our doorstep, and making our best judgments about the potential clients' seriousness of purpose in dealing with their problems and their creditors. It's my good name on the firm's door, and after half a century that reputation is worth more than the revenue from any case—any 10 cases—that might come our way. So I am very careful about whom I let use my name to help solve their financial difficulties. Principals at these first meetings often think *they* are the only ones sizing up the person on the other side of the desk and making the decision about whether a good client / professional match has been found. So it went with Smith and Jones.

It didn't take much to see that Smith and Jones were in the classic tapped-out, hyper-leveraged situation. Not one cash dollar was left to be borrowed from their alleged futures. Smith's and Jones's personal assets had been pledged as collateral for loans. Meanwhile they had operated on the basis of realizing some projected income that did not show up, and—as it turns out—was never going to show up. They had dug themselves a very deep hole. Nonetheless they had serious income that was *not* imaginary or speculative. Time and turmoil and pain were inevitable, all around, but they did not face a career switch to burger-flipping. So I gave them some advice I have had occasion to deliver more times than I can count.

I told Smith and Jones they had a decision to make right now. They could spend a lot of time, grief, and energy trying to save their current business entity, or they could spend it trying to create a new business entity. Either way there would be grief and turmoil. After hearing that advice in a certain amount of detail, Smith and Jones suggested they'd like to keep the same entity in place. I asked them how they proposed to do that while buried so deep in debt. Their grandkids and maybe their kids would be writing monthly checks on their obligations. Thank God, I told them, you're in the United States and in the 21st Century; otherwise you'd be headed to debtors prison for sure, because every additional penny this entity spends will be coming out of your creditors' pockets.

Smith and Jones said the speculative income that failed to show up was their accountant's fault. They asked us for help in drawing up a 90-day business plan that would show their bank they had made initial steps on a long but successful slog back to black ink on their bottom line. We spent more time than we should have—several days—chasing down the viability of what they proposed. That was enough time to discover that my initial quick glance at the balance sheet had revealed the truth. These guys had taken themselves down so far there was no way they could climb back up the slippery slope. What they really wanted was for the bank to see my firm's good name on a business plan that would give Smith and Jones 90 days to perform certain professional/financial maneuvers that would keep their company in business and shield much of their personal assets. Meanwhile, we discovered, they sought to use cash from secured creditors' collateral to pay long-overdue bills to a number of "friendly" unsecured creditors. Under cover of that house of cards they somehow thought I would represent their "good prospects" to the bank. Instead, we parted ways with Smith and Jones without realizing one hour's compensation for our troubles. The bank thanked us for giving a heads-up that a 90-day business plan would *not* be coming from McTevia & Associates. I don't know, at this writing, where Smith and Jones wound up, or whether they found someone willing to help them troll for still more debt.

Let me reiterate. A small minority of people and a small minority of companies have *always* leaped at a chance to slash and burn Dun & Bradstreet's time-tested definition of credit: "Man's confidence in man." Things change. I have never seen that confidence under siege remotely to the extent it is today. Let the quantifiers try to quantify it, if possible. But how does one quantify the fact that, in less than two decades, failing to fulfill an obligation to a creditor has become defined by many business principals as something like: "When things aren't going well for me, an *honest outcome* that is *to be expected*"? Another way to say that would be: "Hey, it's legal, so it must be ethical." It's rampant out there. My professional colleagues will, if polled, affirm that.

In 1834, on the floor of the U.S. Senate, Daniel Webster defined credit as "the vital air of the system of modern commerce." Winding up to full oratorical flourish, Webster intoned: "It (commercial credit) has done more—a thousand times more—to enrich nations than all the mines of the entire world. It has excited labor, stimulated manufactures, pushed commerce over every sea, and brought every nation, every kingdom and every small tribe among the races of men to be known to all the rest. It has raised armies, equipped navies and triumphed over the gross power of mere numbers. It has established national superiority on the foundation of intelligence, wealth and well directed industry."

Considering that the vast majority of business is conducted with credit rather than cash, old Dan Webster certainly had it right. So did Dun & Bradstreet. But I think the good senator and Lewis Tappan, who founded Dun & Bradstreet seven years after Webster's speech, would have a coronary if they could witness a credit card being offered as payment for fast food, or could ponder the reality of a $13,000,000,000,000 national debt, or were given a chance to study the unfunded (and unbudgeted) future financial obligations of our state, local, and national governments. If Webster and Tappan survived their heart problems, it would be interesting to see whether they could find any traction while guesting on today's cable news chatterfests. In truth, I don't think today's U.S. Senate would pay any attention to perhaps its most famous alumnus.

But that sort of thing is where the next chapter will take us.

Here let me remind you that most business principals remain honest men and women. If looking for a chance to give a haircut to a commercial creditor is commonplace, who is to object when homeowners line up to haircut their mortgage holders, and when the U.S. government is positioning itself to give the world the mother of all haircuts? Instead, I'll close out this chapter with an illustration of what "man's confidence in man" is really all about. From my vantage point as a numbers guy navigating the seas of credit, there are compelling stories over every horizon; one can even find heroes. If Hollywood really wanted to save the world from its greatest perils, it might find a way to tell stories like this one.

Over the years I've handled several interesting cases down on the Louisiana bayous. That might seem like a long commute for someone who does most of his work in the Upper Midwest. All business is about people, however, and a banker in my home region who came to respect my skills a great deal found himself working at a New Orleans bank. When his new institution found itself dealing with major troubled loans, I was soon delighted to discover the wonders of coastal Louisiana.

One such case led me into the world of offshore oil drilling, a field almost as specialized as turnaround management. These huge rigs are a world unto themselves—well, a substantial *village* unto themselves. To do a rig's work, several hundred people live miles offshore in living quarters that amount to the largest modular housing units known to man. One of my favorite cases involved a third-generation company that constructed these quarters on shore. Towering cranes on a cargo ship would then lift the entire self-sufficient behemoth—containing everything from bedrooms and kitchens and rec rooms to toilet paper and soap—onto a barge for transport to a completed offshore well. The cargo ship would follow with its cranes, lift the unit onto the rig...and there sat your brand-new petroleum-seeking village.

One such company was a family business that in all those years had never left a horse in the starting gate, had never walked away from an obligation. Having gotten to know them, I can say the walking-away course of action is something this outfit would never have considered. By the time I was called upon to be of assistance, the family was in its third generation of shipping product offshore not just in the Gulf of Mexico, but also the Gulf of Oman, the North Sea, and just about anywhere man extracted oil from beneath water. The family tree had taken root far and wide. Their clients included giant publicly traded oil companies, individual oil tycoons, and sovereign states with drilling operations. The family firm had such an impeccable record of performance reliability that they and their customers had settled into pay-as-you-go arrangements. The firm received progress payments as long as a project moved according to a previously arranged schedule. Everybody was happy.

Then came a big problem with a big project. The

causes were many. Engineering changes brought some delays. A shortage arose in certain materials and components. And there was a labor strike. Red ink began to flow onto the ledger. Even a well-run company can encounter this sort of thing. And even that well-run company will *need* to borrow some serious cash to keep going. Which is where this company sat when the bank brought in McTevia & Associates. We worked with the firm's owners and developed a realistic budget that would see the bad-luck project through to the finish. It was a tough-love financial regimen with lots of cuts, no perks, downsizing, and all the things a realist does to stop spending what he does not have. Despite the company's stellar track record, enough time had been lost that progress payments had disappeared and assembling the big project had become a C.O.D. endeavor. Operating losses during the unpleasantness meant cash on hand had been depleted, and debts to unsecured creditors were mounting. To finish the project, the company would need a bridge loan adding up to millions of dollars. The bank was willing to structure a loan so the company could pay its workers and purchase new materials, but was not at all interested—as the prime secured creditor—in lending money for use in paying off the unsecured creditors (a laudable concept that Smith and Jones had not been willing to accept). Even with the austere financial regimen we prepared, the company would need something more than what the bank was willing, understandably, to offer.

This company had some options. And it was a joy to watch the family choose and execute a course of action. The three founding brothers had all become extremely wealthy, having earned their money in this and related industries for some 75 years. The family's personal assets were huge, but not a penny had been pledged to the bank. There were no personal guarantees of any kind to any of the company's creditors. The various family members could easily have walked away from the business, which would be forced to file for bankruptcy. They could have asked the customer for a haircut or a handout, holding the big project for ransom. They could have breached the contract, leaving the customer (the oil rig's owner and its employees) in deep trouble. But the family did none of those things. In fact, what they did ran against the advice of their accountants and attorneys.

At an all-day family meeting of some 30 people, I explained every option available to them. The family listened, then made its decision. Family members formed a company, funded it with their personal assets, and pledged that company in joint participation with the bank in support of the respected old company until the big project was completed, delivered, and paid for. No horses left in the starting gate with this crew.

You will see in the following quote my best attempt at rendering a bayou drawl. I am quoting him that way because the words he spoke were powerful and so unforgettable I hear the drawl in my mind. The most senior son of one of the three founders addressed the group and said:

"Mr. MacT, we all don't subscribe to fixin' our

problems by settin' them on other folks. That might sound like bad business, but it ain't bad livin', I 'spect. We've got suppliers and folks that have made us rich people that are still workin' for us down in the flats, and we ain't gonna let 'em down just cuz' we got some problems. We ain't gonna cut and run. You bet."

We had that family's company as a client for nearly two years. I wish one of them had run for president of the United States.

6

A Congress of Fools

*What experience and history teach is this—
that people and governments never have
learned anything from history, or acted on
principles deduced from it.*
— Georg Wilhelm Friedrich Hegel,
Philosophy of History.

*Experience keeps a dear school, but fools
will learn in no other.*
— Benjamin Franklin, *Poor Richard's Almanack.*

When I told friends and colleagues about this
book project, most said my timing was *way* off.
Surely, they reasoned, our nation's debt trajectory
would lead to major reforms long before I could put
even one copy into a reader's hands. Surely, they
said, an impending train wreck of this magnitude
would send alarms up and down the line and force
our government to start living within its means.
Surely, and sadly, they could not be more wrong.
Their logic was impeccable. Their sense of urgency
was well-founded. But they did not understand the
depth of this nation's debt addiction. No entity in

the world possesses our government's power to keep doing the wrong thing. While stealing ever more cash from future generations' well-being, the U.S. Congress has built a wondrous levee of denial to hold back the inevitable disaster as long as possible.

When fiscal insanity is allowed to become business as usual, people do things they once could not have imagined themselves doing. You've seen that in the picture I drew of how the ethics of debt management has been corrupted in the business world. In Washington, D.C., the same dynamic is true, except for two things, which seemingly could not occur side by side. First, our government's debt is astronomical and is guaranteed to soar—unless someone stops it—to whatever level lies beyond astronomical. Second, this is happening in plain sight, with your money, but the congressional levee of denial has yet to collapse. As long as the levee holds, mindless borrowing will continue, and the disaster awaiting our grandkids will only be worse. Sometimes it takes an unlikely hero to land a good punch. I think such a hero—however flawed, and however disparaged by news media at the time—emerged on February 25, 2010. If history looks kindly on him only because of a single day's actions, he won't be the first.

Politics and political commentators have a long tradition of shooting any messenger who brings unpopular news, however accurate that news might be. Snipers cannot be happier than when unpopular news is delivered by a messenger who already is mortally wounded. So it went that February day as Jim Bunning, the Hall of Fame pitcher who threw no-hitters in both major leagues, rose to speak on the floor of the U.S. Senate. Bunning, who had represented Kentucky in the Senate since 1999, was spurting blood from countless wounds even before he spoke. In early January he had missed a week of Senate sessions, with no explanation beyond "taking care of a family commitment." Back home his popularity ratings were low, and so were his campaign contributions. In 2004 he had accused his campaign opponent of being "limp-wristed" and looking "like one of Saddam Hussein's sons." Bunning was 78 years old and sometimes forgetful. His opponents on occasion openly accused him of being mentally unbalanced. A month before his February 25th turn on the Senate floor, Bunning had announced he would not run for re-election. A month before that, on Christmas Eve, he was home with his family, making him the only senator who did not cast a vote on the historic Obama health-care reform bill. So Bunning was a lame duck, and he was a dead duck. Never has such an unpopular messenger brought such unpopular, painful, accurate, and vital "news" to the Senate floor.

The Senate on that day was about to approve $10 billion in funding for several federal programs, most visibly an unemployment benefits extension. Bunning supported all the items covered by the legislation, and said so. His heresy was that he wanted to pay the tab rather than put it on the national credit card. "If we can't find $10 billion to pay for something that we all support, we will never pay for anything on the floor of this U.S. Senate," he said. Instead of approving the $10 billion off-budget, Bunning wanted to "pay for it" with unused funds from the 2009 stimulus bill. Even Bunning's heresy was not, of course, anything near cash-and-carry fiscal policy. The budget deficit was approaching $2 trillion. Bunning merely sought to include the $10 billion in that deficit-ridden budget, rather than writing a $10-billion check from a non-existent account with a *zero* balance. As I said, the federal government has remarkable ways of trying to live in the future. "We cannot keep adding to the debt," Bunning plaintively observed. "It's over $14 trillion and going up fast."

I would have expected anyone able to sit up and take nourishment to see the importance and timeliness of Bunning's message. In my view—speaking as someone who avoids spectator sports if there is so much as a crossword puzzle to do instead—Bunning should have been carried off the playing field on the shoulders of his congressional teammates, while millions of Americans cheered. True, the hero of this particular day had in the past voted *for* similarly unfunded expenditures. So what? Every member of Congress—including anyone who approved one dime for the troops in Iraq and Afghanistan—has done so. Many lawmakers will have to make course corrections if the debt insanity ever is to stop. Frankly, I wouldn't have cared *who* stood up in Congress and shouted the truth about the Emperor's new fiscal clothes. It's the message that counts. In this case the messenger drew so much fire that his message was heard by almost no one.

In Congress, most members of Bunning's own party avoided comment. A few sought out TV cameras to distance themselves from the sacrilege of expecting government to become even semi-serious about pay-as-you-go. The other party, of course, chastised Bunning in strong terms. I can't say "strongest possible terms" because that was left for the news media, which played it as nothing more than a story about an old man prone to wacky behavior. After several days of delay, during which no major news organization did any serious reporting about the deficit and the debt, Senate leaders finally allowed a vote on Bunning's proposal to "pay for" the unemployment benefits. Bunning's plea was defeated, 53 to 43. The Senate then overwhelmingly voted to put the $10 billion on its charge card. Lost in a tide of business as usual, an extraordinary "teachable moment" didn't get taught. Many of us, of course, *could* see the wisdom in the old pitcher's message. But even a couple million people don't equate to one percent in a nation of 300 million. The number of Americans genuinely serious about addressing the greatest peril facing our nation still amounts, at this late date, to a trickle. Very few such realists are in government. So no, I don't expect my message will become obsolete before you read these pages. Or, unfortunately, any time soon afterward.

Cursory analysis of the "little" spending bill Bunning sidetracked for a few days would have made a good vehicle for any journalist wishing to report the story of our debt crisis. The jerrybuilt house of credit cards known as federal appropriations comprises an endless process of buying by borrowing. Any individual who spent the way Uncle Sam spends would long ago have seen his credit cards confiscated. By now that individual would have been charged with fraud. Think Bernie Madoff as you read the following paragraph. It's a mere footnote—but a telling one—in the saga of Washington, D.C's, mad rush to insolvency and beyond.

One item in the legislation Bunning stymied briefly was the "doc fix," a regularly scheduled federal fiscal delusion supported by phony bookkeeping. A previous Congress, in a fit of cost-containment, ordered cuts in reimbursement paid to doctors and others who provide health care under Medicare and Medicaid. But as every schoolboy knows, the feds don't pay doctors enough as it is. This means private payers wind up, in effect, subsidizing the federal portion of our health-care system. Consequently, every time reimbursement rates for government-provided health care are scheduled to be lowered by the cost-containment statute, Congress reverses itself and restores the full rate. This is called the "doc fix." Everybody knows the doc fix will happen, as surely as beer will make you belch, whenever a payment reduction is scheduled. And yet, even as Jim Bunning tried in vain to make his point on the Senate floor, the biggest spending bill of this decade—health-care reform—was moving forward under the pretense that the "doc fix" *never* happens.

The Congressional Budget Office, charged with "scoring" the cost of legislation, functions by law like a pollster limited to asking only questions written by his clients. In scoring the cost of a health-care bill, the CBO is required to include the fictional decrease in fees paid to doctors and hospitals. The CBO is not allowed to say: "Hey, we refuse to score this bill as if you'll be saving all that money everyone knows you won't be saving!" Cobble together enough similar phony bookkeeping devices and you have a piece of legislation that beyond question will cost enormously more money—which we don't have—than Congress says it will cost. It happens all the time. Bernie Madoff, unfortunately for him, could not emulate his congressional colleagues by borrowing endlessly or by printing money to make the Ponzi-game balance sheet stay afloat a while longer. If Madoff did have a printing press turning out greenbacks, he would still be out there peddling his wares. Word of mouth would still be touting his Ponzi scheme as a sure thing.

Forget rocket science. This is not even high-school algebra. It is grade-school arithmetic, adult common sense, and a moral willingness to avoid doing the wrong thing even when going wrong is the convenient path. There is no news flash in this chapter, unless it's that no one I know of—including me—can definitively explain why the men and women elected to oversee this once-great nation's treasure are so fiscally incompetent. If we were all assigned to round up the usual suspects, however, my #1 nomination would be this: People do stupid things, or at the very least they do unwise things, with borrowed money incredibly more often than they do stupid or unwise things with their own cash. I have seen this with companies large and small, and with individuals' checkbooks, throughout my career. It is an immutable fact. Peddlers, vendors, and retailers from flea markets to the finest malls regard credit cards as the greatest thing since air and water. Nothing turns a shopper into an aggressive buyer like the ability to pay without finding enough cash in wallet or purse. Some companies with a generous unused line of credit will, if their accounting department and bank allow it, go out and leverage their least-solid schemes and dreams. Force a person or a company to pull cash dollars out of the vault to make a purchase and it is incrementally more likely to be a wise and affordable expenditure. But I digress. Or do I? This book, after all, talks front to back about the corrosive effects of entering into unwise, unwarranted, unchecked debt. The "unsustainable" part of it comes along soon enough.

In any case, the fiscal incompetence of our elected officials reaches an awe-inspiring level, in the full meaning of "awe." The ability to drive a going enterprise so far into the hole is not merely a matter of wonderment, but of *dread*. How could this happen? Most people we send to Washington are smart. Most are sincere in their desire to do good things for their constituents and for the country. Most are well-educated. Perhaps all those qualities are over-ridden by the ability, once in Washington, to borrow money in seemingly endless quantity and to print tons of currency that is, if only for the moment, the world standard. We *know* this is a major piece of the equation that put us where we are. Fiscal irresponsibility has become standard behavior. Meanwhile, fiscal responsibility is seen as deviancy to be derided and, worst of all, ignored. The *New York Times* columnist and Nobel Prize-winning economist Paul Krugman managed to write a piece about Jim Bunning's action without mentioning, not once, Bunning's stated reason for his protest.

Seven months before the Kentuckian's "wacko" appeal for fiscal sanity, the head of the Congressional Budget Office, Douglas Elmendorf, testified to the Senate Budget Committee. Elmendorf told senators: "The federal budget is on an unsustainable path —meaning federal debt will continue to grow much faster than the economy over the long run." Six months later, just a few weeks before Bunning was ridiculed for suggesting lawmakers pay for at least those items they all agreed upon, Elmendorf went over to the other side of the Capitol and testified to the House Budget Committee. He told its members: "I think most observers expect that the government will act; that the unsustainability will be resolved through action, not through witnessing some collapse down the road. If literally nothing is done, then eventually something very, very bad happens. But I think the widespread view is that you and your colleagues will take action." Re-read that last sentence again and you see why I would not hesitate to wager that the message of this book will not become obsolete any time soon. I doubt Doug Elmendorf would want to take my bet, though.

Everything about my message proclaims that individual behavior matters. We are a bottom-up democracy, not a top-down dictatorship. The guy at the top is supposed to represent our will, not vice-versa. The people, not the dictates of a monarch, shape our evolving culture. Our nation's founding documents proclaim nothing if not the ascendancy and eminence of the individual citizen. So it's with good reason that I keep citing the credit-card purchase of fast food as perhaps the iconic American behavior at the dawn of the 21st Century. If I am going to rail against the fiscal incompetence of our *elected* leaders, then how can I not remind that Pogo's insightful observation will *always* be insightful: "We have met the enemy, and he is us."

It's also true, though, that a basic common-sense rule for authors would go something like: "Don't keep beating up on your readers or they'll toss your book in the trash and go somewhere they won't be assaulted on every page." I obviously do not want you to abandon these pages. And I obviously have your grandchildren as much in mind as my own grandchildren when I ring the alarm bell so loudly. Besides, the chicken-and-the-egg factor flows throughout the debt-disaster equation, no? To cite just the most obvious example from the 2008–2009 meltdown, do you want to blame the subprime mortgage mess on people with lousy credit or low incomes who nonetheless were offered deals on houses they had no business buying? Should we beat up on *them*? Well, yeah. Sort of. A little bit. If they really understood what they were doing. Remember what I just said about people doing stupid things with borrowed money? But what about the lender who wrote the mortgage, the guy who is supposed to be the pro when it comes to such matters? And what about the institution further up the food chain who said, "Let's take a big bundle of these ridiculous mortgages and find a way to market them as if they were blue-chip stocks." What about another institution—or maybe a branch of the *same* institution—that says: "Hey, let's figure out a way to bet that all those 'blue-chip' equities based on mortgages no Podunk 1950s bank manager ever would have written *will go belly up*."

The fact is, in my adult lifetime we—individuals, institutions, governments—have used technology and rampant consumerism to build a *debt culture* that would be abhorrent to every previous generation of Americans. To my mind this is more threatening to our society's well-being and survival than any real or imagined misreading of the founders' intent regarding guns or abortion or taxes or pre-emptive wars or any other conversational hot button. Hop in your time machine. Bring along a balance sheet outlining our government's current debt and future statutory obligations. Set the machine to 1800 and push the button. Show that shameful mess to Franklin or Washington or Jefferson or Adams. Don't say a word. See what kind of response you get. Fast forward to Lincoln's day. Hand Abe the balance sheet and ask whether the union he fought to keep in one piece has managed, in his opinion, to bankrupt itself. I think we know their answers. And even though the individual does indeed matter in our representative democracy, let me assure any ordinary citizen reading my book: I don't hold you personally responsible for our $13-trillion nightmare.

Look at it this way. Here's another index of contemporary America's unique ability to mismanage debt. Early in 2010 more than 11 million American families were underwater on their home mortgages. With the average U.S. household most recently measured to be 2.59 persons, that's 28 million Americans living in a house that is worth less than the amount owed on the mortgage. Nearly everyone is aware of that phenomenon, but few look beyond the personal impact of these numbers and get seriously worried about the implications for our society. This is one instance where events might in fact race past my narrative before you read it. So let me just say it will be interesting to see how Main Street banks, as opposed to Wall Street banks, fare in the coming year or two. And to see what it means when millions of people in our "mobile society" are rendered immobile, tethered to a dead weight they thought was a "sure investment." And to see how much iceberg lies below the surface of the economic "recovery" that is rumored at least once a week. And to see whether the ultimate solution for an underwater home "owner"—walking away from financial obligation—might also loom as the ultimate solution for the biggest debtor of all.

In any case, if you are reading this book while living in an underwater house, it is pretty clear that society is not beating you up and blaming you for the mess. Brett Arends, a *Wall Street Journal* columnist, surveyed the carnage from an underwater perspective in February 2010 and declared that "walking away from debts is as American as apple pie." A month earlier, Roger Lowenstein wrote in the *New York*

Times magazine: "No one says defaulting on a contract is pretty or that, in a perfectly functioning society, defaults would be the rule. But to put the onus for restraint on ordinary homeowners seems rather strange." Both writers make a pragmatically valid 21st Century point. Default has become the American way—though very few are yet bold enough to talk about the mother of all defaults that *must* come if Jim Bunning's pitch for fiscal integrity continues to be derided as the meaningless rant of a doddering old man.

Arends's column analyzed the arithmetic faced by Americans whose homes are seriously underwater, and then gave a well-drafted, concise version of the financial advice buzzing through countless McMansion subdivisions. You have no equity to be preserved. It might be many years, if ever, before your home's value so much as equals your mortgage debt. During those years your payments could be building assets instead of being frittered away. Meanwhile, it's not *your* home, not even a piece of it. You are renting it from the bank at inflated rates. The legal consequences of walking away? Check with your lawyer, Arends urged; but any consequences are likely to be less than you think, perhaps none at all. Banks are so inundated with this problem that many won't even come after you. You say you are so old-fashioned that you see a moral problem with turning deadbeat...with straying so incredibly far from the old ideal of the mortgage-burning party? Hey, haven't you been reading the papers? *The economy is fundamentally immoral.* Besides, Arends noted, businesses have always used limited liability to protect themselves; you shouldn't be ashamed to do so yourself.

One fine point of this ethical quandary flooding the new wetlands of home ownership is the distinction between a house-poor, wiped-out citizen who cannot afford the bleed of paying on an overvalued mortgage, and someone who *can* afford "inflated rent payments." For the latter, an ethically quaint phrase—"strategic default"—quickly replaced the irresponsible-sounding "walk away from the mortgage." I can't quarrel generally with the advice found in Arends's column and elsewhere. But without trying to impersonate a lawyer (which I am not), or feigning knowledge of any individual situation (which I don't have), I would caution that buying a house almost always entails not just a mortgage but a promissory note. Cheerfully handing a bank your house keys while planning to start over down the road does *not* satisfy that note. Banks these days have plenty on their plates other than going into the full-time business of asking courts for default judgments and collecting on them. That is why—*generally* speaking—banks stand ready to deal with someone who is solvent despite living in an underwater home. That's a good environment in which to ask a bank to split the pain of home "value" that disappeared into thin air. Without that banker's blessing, one should not forget that promissory notes do not also vanish into thin air unless you have nothing left with which to fulfill your promise. If you do, the bank can come and get it. Or can sell the note to someone else. Do not be surprised—ah, the dark humor of the idea—if someone starts bundling such notes as investment products.

Interesting to note that McDonald's began accepting credit-card payment for a $5 bag of burgers at company-owned restaurants in 2004, less than five years before so many $500,000 McMansions slipped underwater. If this book were a journalistic effort rather than a memoir from a profession I still practice, I'm sure I could with little difficulty find a pile of personal bankruptcies in which the tapped-out individual's charge-card addiction included a habit of swiping, so to speak, drive-through treats for the kids. Looking at those charge slips, I guess one could say these folks walked away from a Happy Meal.

One person who predictably voiced a negative view about "walking away" was John Courson, CEO of the Mortgage Bankers Association. Late in 2009 he told an interviewer that underwater mortgage borrowers should keep making their house payments. Courson noted that defaults hurt neighborhoods by lowering property values, and rhetorically asked: "What about the message they will send to their family and their kids and their friends?" But a few months later, just days before Arends's column declared walking away from debts to be "as American as apple pie," the Mortgage Bankers Association sold its three-year-old headquarters located in—where else?—Washington, D.C. The association had bought the building for $79 million, with $4 million down. That's only about one-fourth the standard down payment that prevailed in my young adult days. Neither John Courson nor anyone else at the association would say how big a haircut the group gave its lenders while unloading the building (even 10-story structures go underwater) for just $41 million. "We're not going to discuss the financing," Courson told the *Wall Street Journal*. The Mortgage Bankers Association, meanwhile, went looking for rented quarters in the town that—speaking of "the message they will send to their family and their kids and their friends"—manages our national debt.

Two questions come quickly to mind.

First, who could possibly quarrel with the analysis in Arends's column analysis? The Mortgage Bankers Association, a professional group that cheerleads for ethics in the lending business, gave its own lenders a haircut. What's next? A bank-robbery gang led by FBI agents?

Second, I'm quite sure a substantial number of philosophers fervently believe the economy in which I grew up and cut my professional teeth was also "fundamentally immoral." But can anyone look at future generations' deepening peril and say fiscal ethics today are no different than when people held mortgage-burning parties after years of making double payments to get "free and clear"? Answer: Some people say the Earth is flat. Our elected representatives seem capable of believing the Earth is flat, and believing that someone who stands on the Senate floor to declare otherwise has lost touch with reality. Or maybe the vast majority of Jim Bunning's congressional detractors knew the old boy's little speech was precisely correct. The spineless and the opportunistic always stand ready, willing, and able to say and do things they don't really believe in.

Blame for theft of this country's future treasury and well-being can indeed be found at addresses along Main Street, Wall Street, Pennsylvania Avenue, and all connecting streets. No doubt about it. Ordinary Americans got personally comfortable with the fiscal and moral disaster of spending non-existent wealth that, if and when it materializes, belongs to their unborn descendants. Business and industry got into a similarly insane relationship with the future, obsessed with leveraging instant growth—real or imagined. But this does *not* make it fair to say...it is in fact ludicrous to say: "Hey, politicians are *supposed* to reflect the lives and goals of their constituents. You say government is maxing out its credit, and will walk away from its own countless, huge, unfunded promises? What's your beef? That's the American way of life." Sorry, no. That equation isn't acceptable. It's not for nothing that we call our elected officials "leaders." They are supposed to lead us upward, not downward.

No individual or company, no matter how wealthy or vital, can drag the United States, and perhaps much of the world, into the abyss by going belly up. But 535 Americans—a small enough number to qualify for a federal small-business loan—*can* "achieve" exactly that. The voting members of the U.S. House and Senate (of either party), especially when aided and abetted by the White House (in the hands of either party), have accelerated our runaway debt to a speed that would dazzle even the Star Trek crew. Yes, individual behavior matters. But this book was not written because Grandpa George and Great-Grandma Ellen are foolishly trying to live in the future and are squandering the family treasure. This book was written because *scores of millions* of as-yet-unborn Americans—a generation or two, at least—are going to suffer at the hands of voting majorities among 100 senators and 435 representatives. By refusing to acknowledge the difference between present and future, Congress has led our government hell-bent down a path that leads to a brutal destination. Always. A very painful outcome for our fiscally troubled nation has become inevitable.

The history of *every* fiscally troubled entity in my long professional experience—which, like any career, breeds knowledge greater than the sum of its parts—leaves me with no doubt about this outcome. Forgive me for not being an economist or a philosopher or even a journalist—and certainly not a politician—but I do believe fiscal trajectories and outcomes I have witnessed are important. This country's balance sheet shouts out that American society is in store for, at best, tears and pain followed by a *long* period of healing and repair. That's the best-case scenario. Sad to say, those Americans who will endure by far the greatest suffering for the longest time will have had nothing to do with causing that fate. Their suffering already has been guaranteed, a miserably upside-down birthright. There is wiggle room to debate the suffering's severity (life-threatening or "merely" critical)...to debate the precise point in time the runaway debt train will at last jump the tracks...to debate how long it might then take to get our economy and society back to whatever best shape the debt-bombed generations can manage. But why debate such things? Wouldn't any sane person instead move immediately to do whatever possible to ensure the least pain and fewest possible casualties? Of course. Which is why the collective fiscal behavior of the United States Congress has been, and continues to be, not merely incompetent but also insane. That is indeed an amazing thing to say; but how else can one regard what our leaders have done to our grandchildren's futures?

When I personally delivered a copy of *Bankrupt* to every congressman in spring 1993, friends told me I was tilting windmills. The Prologue to this book amounts to an essay illustrating how right those friends were. Congress was not at all interested in the message. The years soon after *Bankrupt* produced, coincidentally, a moment of false fiscal sanity that was in truth a smoke-and-mirrors show. A very brief history of America's finances before, during, and after that blip does nothing to alter my "insane" diagnosis. The unique intersection of Bill Clinton's and Newt Gingrich's careers was the political quotient of the famous Clinton-era balanced budget. There was also the dot.com quotient—an unexpected revenue boost from the, well, *insane* era when internet startup companies invested their entire capitalization in Super Bowl commercials (to be followed by the dot.com bust). There was also an intersection of demographics and payroll taxes in which Social Security revenues surpassed current

Social Security outlays (kiss that one goodbye). There was also an income-tax increase. And the overall economy was good, a piece of serendipity Democrats claim for Clinton and Republicans claim for Clinton's predecessor—a dispute that means nothing here, either way.

The smoke and mirrors I see in what some now describe as a Golden Age for budgetary sanity are these:

First, and most basically, deficits are one thing and debt is another. No one got serious about the debt, interest on the debt, and getting rid of that anchor in anticipation of *future* bad situations. Any principal in even a storefront business understands how that works. So should our government. Did the feds find it necessary to "raise capital" any time soon after 1999? Do you think? How has that gone?

Second, you might say, "Hey, if revenues were up because of good times and tax *rates* were up besides, and no one took a run at paying down the debt, then somebody must have been spending big-time." You bet. Both political parties poured new money, then and now, into the very entitlement programs that everyone knows—and has known for decades— represent the girth of the fiscal elephant in America's living room.

Third (see above), why should it even matter that for a moment Social Security revenues exceeded current expenditures? Shouldn't that little surplus have been applied against the train wreck we all knew was about to happen? Isn't letting America's elderly believe in a "Social Security trust fund" a fraud that would have made P.T. Barnum jealous?

Fourth, no one should ever be allowed within 100 miles of Washington if he or she does not understand and admit that projections of any federal program's future costs are conservative, often wildly conservative...that statutes themselves are loaded with phony economies (see "doc fix" above)...that built-in future budget implosions, though obvious to all, will be ignored until they suck the oxygen out of the moment. For the latter, see not only Social Security, Medicare, and Medicaid, but also this benign, bureaucratic, but very concrete word, "infrastructure." Not only am I not a lawyer, economist, philosopher, journalist, or politician—I am also not an engineer. But how many college degrees are required to understand the fiscal meaning of the following quote from a 2007 MIT Faculty Newsletter, before the Great Recession officially began: "Most of our road, rail, water, sewer, electric power, wired telephone, and other distributed systems infrastructure are old and in need of repair. Our ports, airports, and rail terminals are archaic, ill designed, badly run, and poorly maintained." Two years later, the national engineering society estimated our infrastructure *needed* more than *$2 trillion* worth of repairs within five years.

In a sane world, in touch with reality, one takes care of these things by making room in budgets to retire debt or set aside funds (preferably both), not by sucking up all revenues available. Budgetary discipline not only frees up cash for vital projects, it also assures access to reasonable levels of credit (new debt) in unusual times. In other words, any good-times balanced budget that doesn't seriously pursue debt reduction and doesn't account for impending needs is *not* a symptom of a fiscal Golden Age. It's a symptom of unnecessarily and foolishly living in the future (which as you have figured out, really means living high in the *present* by stealing from anyone unfortunate enough to still be around in the future).

So, yes; "insane" has been my diagnosis for federal fiscal policy during nearly my entire adult life. Democratic insanity and Republican insanity. This has amazed me almost as long as I can remember. Lately, as I have said, my thoughts about it all have swung more toward awe. Even as my view on these matters becomes less and less lonely, Congress finds it impossible to round up a majority in favor of fiscal reality, and in favor of our grandchildren's children. Our lawmakers can easily be swayed to feel compassion for, say, a thumbnail-sized species of lizard found only in one southern county, and will spend a few million dollars that allegedly will keep that lizard on the planet a while longer. Our government routinely spends billions on programs speculated to benefit people on the other side of the Earth who don't like us very much, then pays the tab by dipping into future generations' treasure. Closer to home, our society is being driven to bankruptcy by flawed entitlement programs that Congress for decades has been terrified to repair. It all will end very badly. Our "leaders" remain deer in the headlights of this runaway train. That is beyond amazing or even awesome. It is dreadful. It is insane.

Some who camp on my side of this great divide are, as they say, outliers. Take Ron Paul, for instance. Many of the Texas congressman's contributions to the public debate have been spot-on. I don't say this as a political endorsement. I don't endorse anyone. I don't even care to say who I vote for. But in February 2010, when CNN's Wolf Blitzer asked Congressman Paul if he agreed that the government was "broken," Paul's response ignited the kind of fire that takes hold whenever serious fiscal problems get discussed seriously.

As for government being "broken," a popular term in the wake of the 2008-2009 meltdown, Paul replied: "It certainly is. I might define it a little bit differently. I think the mechanism is broken because the government is *broke*, and that's a big difference. When you have a lot of money you can be inefficient, and you can do things. Everybody gets what they want. But once a government becomes broke and the people are really broke too, because there are not enough people working to feed the cow, then there's this inefficiency...The government is too big, it's already very inefficient, and that is the reason we actually met this bankruptcy. I don't think we can solve this until we admit the bankruptcy and do something about it—which means you cut way back..."

That was enough to bring even Blitzer, a very fair interviewer as TV newscasters go, practically up out of his chair: "Wait a minute! Congressman, you want to see the U.S. government, the American taxpayer, in effect go bankrupt?"

Paul responded: "Well, you have to admit you can't pay the bills. Once the government gets as much debt as we have, you have to liquidate. You can't avoid it. I'm not advising that we renege on paying Treasury bills and sending out Social Security (checks)...but what is going to happen is the debt will be liquidated by paying back money that doesn't have as much value. All you have to have is a 10 percent inflation rate and you have wiped off a trillion dollars worth of debt..."

Such issues are, of course, the very real prospects that should be central to any serious discussion about our fiscal mess. Congressman Paul, outlier or not, had gone straight to the heart of the matter rather than waltzing around it. This led Blitzer to jump in and say: "Oh! That would be unacceptable! Most people's life savings would be lost in that kind of situation within a few years."

Paul said: "That's why we must avoid it."

With that, the red-hot topic was changed immediately. But credit Blitzer and Paul—especially Paul—for at least broaching an adult, if most often avoided, topic. Blitzer interviewed Paul just two days before Bunning took to the Senate floor and made his similar warning. Future historians will be noting, I believe, that *two* outliers made near-simultaneous and notable statements on behalf of fiscal sanity.

If Ron Paul and Jim Bunning are a little too *outlying* for your taste, try this cover story, which also went to the heart of the matter in plain public view:

HOW GREAT POWERS FALL

Steep debt, slow growth, and high spending kill empires—and America could be next

I mentioned that story in passing earlier. But this is a good place to remind that it did not appear in some obscure pamphlet assembled by a small-government fringe group. This was the cover of *Newsweek* (in this case Pearl Harbor Day—December 7, 2009), which is as mainstream as it gets. One would have thought Harvard economist Niall Ferguson's essay, trumpeted on the front of a leading newsmagazine, would be exactly the kind of vehicle to gain traction with our leaders and 24/7 talking heads. Not that *Newsweek* or any other piece of the entire news media establishment could turn this crisis around on a dime. But look at some of the points Ferguson laid out:

- Congress's checkbook management problems have a world-wide reach. "But if the United States succumbs to a fiscal crisis, as an increasing number of economic experts fear it may, then the entire balance of global economic power could shift."

- The article appeared as Congress, and the public, debated President Obama's lingering decision on sending troops to Afghanistan. Ferguson wrote: "In reality, his indecision about the deficit could matter much more for the country's long-term national security."

■ "There is no end in sight to the borrowing binge. *Unless entitlements are cut or taxes are raised, there will never be another balanced budget.*"

■ One rational analysis of current trends foresees that in 20 years as much as seven percent of our total Gross Domestic Product could be devoted *to servicing debt owed to other nations.*

■ Paul Krugman, the Nobel-winner who wrote about Jim Bunning without mentioning why Bunning did what he did, had written in 2003 that "politicians will eventually be tempted to resolve the (fiscal) crisis the way irresponsible governments usually do: by printing money, both to pay current bills and to inflate away debt." To which Ferguson wrote: "Seems pretty reasonable to me." And to which I would note: "Sounds an awful lot like Ron Paul."

■ A rising percentage of federal revenues devoted to federal interest payments, and a declining percentage spent on national defense, appear inevitable. "And history suggests that once you are spending as much as one-fifth of your revenues on debt service, you have a problem."

The *Newsweek* piece ended this way: "Call it the fatal arithmetic of imperial decline. Without radical fiscal reform, it could apply to America next." As handwriting on the wall goes, try overlaying that sentence with this final sentence from a January 2010 column from a different commentator: "What the looming fiscal crisis of this country portends is nothing less than a test of whether this democratic republic is sustainable." That one is from the conservative columnist Pat Buchanan.

So the message of fiscal reality in these dire times can be found all over the place if you look for it. Unlike 1992, when I wrote *Bankrupt*, the message attracts a certain amount of interest. A small minority of Americans even regard it as an urgent subject. Without action, however, an idea is merely an idea. Every member of Congress, for instance, speaks of fiscal reality as a fine thing. They don't, however, produce collective action to make the idea meaningful. Not even when the future viability of their country, the only thing they should care about at the end of the day, lies in the balance. Talking about the problem without doing anything is just another brick in the levee of denial.

The wrongheadedness of Congress on fiscal issues has been rivaled only by the news media's lack of serious interest in the subject. Especially broadcast news, which for more and more Americans *is* "the news." Wink-and-nudge happy talk among anchorpersons, for instance, dismissed the Jim Bunning moment into nothing more than a wacko senior-citizen slice of life. It was the perfect story for late-night comedy masquerading as news, and then being recycled the next day on actual news shows. Another example: For months, most commentators displayed no clue about fiscal sanity's role in attracting interest in the "Tea Party." The very idea of living within our means seems to be, for many in mainstream media, an amusing concept.

I do have some ideas about how our government got, and remains, so far out of touch with fiscal reality. We'll be discussing that. But I thought it imperative to devote one chapter to singling out the 535 members of our nation's two most revered institutions. They are, in my view, very near to completing the destruction of our future prosperity and global stature, not through noble social programs or international gestures, but via the gut-simple route of driving us all into bankruptcy.

Because of them, when we turn to the obligatory chapter on solutions it will largely be a question of: Can the United States reorganize and restructure its incredible fiscal mess and move forward, along the lines of my professional work for many years? Or will it be more like my profession in recent years, where increasingly there is nothing to do but steer a bankrupt entity—and its constituents—toward the softest possible landing for the inevitable liquidation?

No point in talking about solutions to a behavioral problem, though, before talking about what got us into it. So let's first talk about greed, the usefulness of pain, and how easy it is to avoid solving problems when solutions can be delayed (and problems worsened). That may not sound like a numbers guy talking; but believe me, those are the most important issues I have been seeing every day for half a century. The numbers part is easy. The rest is more difficult. If it weren't, even Congress probably would have done the right thing long ago.

7

Life, Liberty and the Pursuit of... Debt?

In our culture, we have become used to an attitude in which economic motivations, relationships, and conventions are fundamental; the language of the seller and customer has wormed its way into practically all areas of our social life, even education and health care. The implication is that the most basic interaction between one human being and another is the carefully calibrated exchange of material resources."

> — Rowan Williams, 104th Archbishop of Canterbury, writing in the January 29, 2010, issue of *Newsweek* after attending a conference at Trinity Wall Street on "Building an Ethical Economy."

So how did we wind up in this mess? What happened? We are a young country, but we've been around for a few centuries. Why now? Greed, after all, is not news. Adam and Eve had everything they wanted except an apple, and we know what happened there. I suspect the first pre-human to climb down from a tree and pick up a club as a hunting weapon almost immediately looked around for a second club to carry in his other hand. I further suspect that if science could somehow verify my suspicion, we would find the ultimate predecessor of the two-car garage. And then, of course, the four-car garage.

Except for a statistically insignificant number of current eccentrics and future saints, everyone is a materialist to some degree. We enjoy our creature comforts and our toys. But there is materialism, and then there is materialism. There is greed, and then there is greed. In the mere span of my adult life I have watched major erosion of our reasonable and sane relationship with the natural desire to acquire *stuff*. Not every American, of course, has moved to the deep end of that drowning pool. Many Americans enjoy lives that are not defined by the stuff in their garages, closets, home entertainment centers, and Sunbelt time-shares. Furthermore, their personal balance sheets are at peace with fiscal reality. Clearly, though, they are a minority and a long way from being trend-setters as defined by the commercial drumbeat in media new and old—and by the fiscal policies of our elected leaders.

If you can remember the 1950s, you have watched America flip-flop from a majority living in the present to a majority living in the future. Saving money used to mean socking away cash for future needs, not "saving money" by maxing out your plastic at sale prices. The fable of the grasshopper's mindless summer of revelry and the ant's hard-working preparation for winter sounds quaint and obscure when told in today's America. If Aesop were around to edit the same thrifty tale for 2010, the fiscal-realist ant would still be able to keep his home in winter no matter the economic carnage raging outside. Unfortunately, the ant's home's value would have plunged along with the house next door occupied by the no-money-down-and-spend-all-your-paycheck grasshopper, who is about to walk away from his mortgage—helping sink the ant's home value even lower. That's a micro view. In a macro view, the federal government's own grasshopper finances are overextended to Mars and back, meaning grandchild ants and grandchild grasshoppers alike will face a depleted and perhaps dangerous future. Most experts on such things, Aesop would note with a tear in his eye, believe we are looking at the very first generation of American grandkids that will be able to look back and say Grandpa was, all his life, better off.

For years I've bemoaned how our debt-addicted society had allowed the living-in-the-future grasshopper to replace the fiscal-realist ant as our role model. Mostly my observation has been met with that "quaint" or "obsolete" label. Recently, though, as the Boomers begin to get their mortality check—and as everyone else takes full notice of how many Boomers there are—more commentators have turned to old Aesop for their metaphors. Some even talk about the Greatest Generation having been succeeded by the Grasshopper Generation. Maybe at the individual level a movement back toward fiscal sanity will be a little quicker and a little broader than I expected. That would be nice. Getting our government to join such a happy trend in a timely manner would be even nicer. And a pipe dream.

No doubt many societies throughout history have succumbed to an irrational, overwrought quest for wealth and its trappings. We are not the first sovereign nation to want it all and want it now *even if we can't afford it*. But thanks to a toxic sandwich of consumerism, easy credit and runaway debt, we have created still another first for world history. Today's America totters on the edge of becoming the first great *democracy* to tumble into the deepest, darkest corners of a greed-driven sovereign debt nightmare. It's the democracy angle that makes our looming fiscal catastrophe unique compared with the list of empires that crumbled under the weight of overreaching debt. *We the people* are the sovereigns here. It's not one emperor or a tiny moneyed class charting our course for fiscal hell. Americans of every economic and social class have been fiscally fiddling, or at the very least sending world-class fiddlers to Washington, while the nation burns.

This broad base of our fiscal mess makes it much more complicated. It also makes Pogo spot-on, as always, with his identification of the enemy as "us." Any fiscal coward or fiscal incompetent who gets voted back to Washington again and again and again obviously represents the fiscal ethic of enough voters to keep his or her job. Both chambers of Congress really ought to crank up the amplifiers and blare out Queen's anthem to greed while voting to spend another boxcar of non-existent money. One assumes a majority of constituents back home will rock along as long as they are able. The roots of our debt disaster, after all, are deeply democratic (small "d"—we are witnessing a bipartisan crime). It's about our entire culture, as Pogo understood. But by all means let's not lose sight of who is in the cab of this runaway train, holding the throttle wide open. They are well-intentioned men and women, which as we all know makes them board-certified for paving the road to hell. In truth, when one spends non-existent money, it doesn't matter whether one spends it on well-intentioned good deeds or loses it at the racetrack. There are consequences. For a person or for a government.

The 535 members of the U.S. House and Senate, aided and abetted by the executive branch, bear responsibility for mismanaging human history's largest purse strings. I am sure every one of them was thinking good thoughts while putting the "tr" in "billions." But they have managed the republic's checkbook with all the discipline of a demented, strung-out, shop-till-you-drop mall maven. Congress sets out each day with the mother of all shopping lists, a scribbled mishmash of impulse items defying imagination, quantification, or rationalization. In November 2004, for instance, after failing to pass annual appropriations bills for a dozen government departments and major agencies, Congress tossed all those pieces of legislation into one stew pot. The way 535 cooks stirred this concoction was wonderfully chronicled by Ken Silverstein in the July 2005 issue of

Harper's Magazine. The piece of legislation Silverstein wrote about was glued together in 72 hours and ran to 3,320 pages. Not one Representative or Senator could possibly have read those pages before enacting them into law, by overwhelming majorities in both houses. Consider the following math. Our honorable elected officials draped this legislation with *11,722* separate earmarks—by now a common term for local pork-barrel projects. If a lawmaker stayed awake for three days and did nothing but read these shopping-list items, he would have to digest more than two earmarks per minute. These earmarks alone added up to $16 billion—equal to the entire Gross Domestic Product of Ghana or Bolivia.

As Congress tossed its $16 billion worth of impulse purchases into the national shopping cart and reached for our national credit card, our national debt seriously began its climb into the stratosphere. The vast majority of these lawmakers were still in office four years later when the subprime earthquake jolted our nation's fiscal house of cards. These same lawmakers were still on hand another two years down the road to deride Jim Bunning for suggesting the world's allegedly greatest legislative body ought to at least pretend it is paying up front for those items everybody agrees are worth buying. And they were still there just two months later when Doug Elmendorf, the Congressional Budget Office Director, once again drew very little attention when he warned that the United States will be in a serious jam if Congress does not cut spending, or increase taxes, or—probably—both. Shucks, imagine that! See

earlier sections of this book regarding the only three
things (decrease expenditures, increase revenues,
and probably both) that can be done in the face of
a financial crisis. See, for that matter, *Bankrupt*,
which I personally delivered to all 535 Senators and
Representatives in 1993. Good luck, Mr. Elmendorf.

The vast majority of the same lawmakers who
approved that 2004 appropriations nightmare are
still drawing paychecks for a job that is supposed to
include caretaking our republic in trust for future
generations. Instead, they continue to simmer and
serve huge vats of credit-card stew. As each vat
is delivered, the legislative chefs step before TV
cameras and earnestly congratulate themselves
for their "hard work." Anyone who hangs ceiling
drywall, works on a factory floor, or holds three
part-time jobs that don't add up to one full-time job
might quarrel with that description. But I digress,
perhaps because it is so tempting and so easy to
place *all* blame for our historic and potentially
fatal fiscal crisis entirely on our elected leaders. In
great measure they deserve it because, as the sign
on Harry Truman's desk suggested, the buck has to
stop somewhere. A Congress that blithely swipes our
credit card for billions of dollars per purchase is as
good a place as any. Any short-term attempt to avert
the worst possible end game *must* start with getting
Congress to throttle down that runaway train. Any
attempt to downsize government's shopping list so
it matches the checkbook (and leaves something for
debt service) *must* start with Congress.

But getting our living-in-the-future society

back in touch with fiscal reality, and answering the "What happened?" question, goes deeper than sending a relief crew down to Washington. I suppose our lawmakers *would* return to fiscal sanity on the day a majority of voters and institutions driving the economy did the same. Meantime, at this writing, Congress is borrowing 40 cents for every dollar it spends. How ironic that one is tempted to quote John Maynard Keynes, the economist in whose name countless barrels of government red ink have been spilled: "In the long run, we're dead." In fact, my career experience tells me that if there is any hope of at least reducing our grandkids' bad fortunes, we need to sprint full-bore toward black ink. We need our leaders to *lead*, and to make a course correction even before our culture's fiscal ethic gets that long-term overhaul. This marathon run of living ever deeper into the future by spending future generations' money must end. Right now.

I'm sure that if 10 reviewers were to write about this book, at least nine would describe my message—whether in praise or scorn– as "simple." I entirely agree. The humorist Robert Benchley wrote: "There are two kinds of people in the world: those who divide the world into two kinds of people, and those who don't." And I am here to tell you, despite Benchley's wit and wisdom, there are two additional kinds of people in the world—those who believe debt has consequences, and those who don't. Simple? You bet. Too simple? I don't think so. In fact, 50 years of refereeing the unavoidable and immutable consequences of unrealistic debt allow me to *know* otherwise. I invite anyone in our poll-crazy news media to go survey everyone who does what I do for a living. They'll *all* tell you that if it weren't for unrealistic debt none of us could have found one billable hour to pursue in our line of work. In short, anyone—congressperson, policy advisor, editorialist, talk-show host, average voter—who thinks an endlessly growing mountain of debt can be passed along to the next generation and beyond without desperate consequences is deluded. Badly so. Dangerously so.

That pile of debt matters, even in a nation that generates—at least for a while longer—the world's greatest economy. What if your grandchild or great-grandchild wakes up one morning as an adult to discover that half the money he sends to Washington will be wasted on servicing an ever-growing debt for projects sent to the landfill before he was born? What if fiscal insanity has been kicked in his direction so long that our single biggest expenditure has become nothing but *interest* on the debt? Insurrection easily occurs to me as one possible result. At the very least, some kind of "peaceful revolution" would seem likely. What would *you* do if you were just entering adult life and woke up to such a fiscal nightmare? I am being kind and conservative in guessing such possibilities. In fiscal 2009 it cost less to borrow money than at any time in your life—but Washington paid out $381 billion in interest. What do you suppose are the odds that the cost of borrowing money might someday be more expensive than *the lowest it has ever been*? If you are a young reader, a nightmare scenario—perhaps the only thing that finally will generate a meaningful public conversation about debt—threatens not just your grandkids, but your sons and daughters. In fact, the percentage of Washington's expenditures going toward nothing but interest on debt might soar high enough and soon enough to make *you* wake up with a profoundly changed attitude toward a country you always have loved.

On the day young Americans wake up to discover someone siphoned their prosperity *into the past*, it will be no consolation to reminisce about days when our society lived in the present and did not steal from the future. Perhaps the victimized new generation, when not preoccupied with survival, will pay no attention to Grandpa's recollection of fiscal sanity but will reinvent that wheel on its own. Why not? Fiscal sanity isn't a difficult concept. Besides, there will be no choice, finally, except to reel society within its means. The byproduct of that step back into sanity—pain—will be everywhere. Feel free, in fact, to circle the following sentence and confront me with it as far into the future as I am lucky enough to remain alive. This society already has managed to live so far into the future, stealing so much from future generations, there *will* be an enormous amount of pain no matter how and when this debt disaster plays out.

The header at the top of this chapter suggests we are talking about greed. I don't know a better one-word explanation for what has happened. Certainly governments and individuals don't behave on perfectly parallel tracks, even in a democracy. But greed is greed. When an ordinary citizen tosses his paycheck and the full faith of his credit-card down a rat hole, it's not an action born in committee meetings and subcommittee meetings. Sales clerks do not lobby him with four-star dinners and golf outings to Bermuda. He cannot, on a trip to the store for bread and milk, scribble "entire tenderloin," "lawn tractor," and "retractable sun shade for deck" onto a shopping list, call them earmarks, and write the cashier a worthless check. If consumerism did work that way, in a maze of parliamentary procedure and special interests, our imaginary shopper would still be one greedy citizen. And when a lawmaker approves the most selfless, altruistic, humanitarian programs, that is also greed if it does not pass the Jim Bunning test. Better yet, let's give it the following test. Let's flash forward to one of those great-grandkids who are going to detest their elders, and maybe detest their country. Let's awaken this young man early one morning and ask: "Hey, your government helped out so-and-so..." and here you can plug any noble but unfunded program that helped bury this kid. Then ask him: "Now don't you feel a whole lot better?"

The Archbishop of Canterbury's quote rings true and is well worth noting. It seems like we *do* these days use dollar signs to keep score in every area of life. But in the arena of fiscal ethics and morals, I'd like to focus tightly on an important distinction that has gotten lost in our time. That is, the cornerstone of fiscal morality and ethics lies not with how we spend money, or how important money is to us, but with making sure we do not spend money we do not possess, or can ever hope to possess. I am amazed this simple guideline is ignored, especially when we are surrounded by proof of why it is so important and so true. Americans used to understand and follow this truth as sure as kids used to play ball in vacant lots. Bankruptcy, once something to be avoided at all costs but now almost a way of life, is about spending money you don't have. Eagerness to give a creditor the shortest possible haircut, as if shopping for the best deal on a used car, strikes me as the epitome of fiscal immorality. Flat-out lying, pretending, arrogating, and assembling virtual wealth you don't really have, then *spending* it, taking real wealth from others while walking away from your mess...that, I think, is the Super Bowl of greed.

Greed comes in many flavors, not all of which can necessarily be sorted, like dirty laundry, into a pile labeled "root of our national crisis." If someone has a ton of money, flaunts it, pays cash to accumulate lots of "stuff" he doesn't need, but doesn't spend beyond his means and therefore does not wind up harming his family or anyone else—then our only real concern is that he has good taste in all that *stuff* he buys. He is greedy, but so what? There's a difference between ethics and esthetics. He might even be helping the economy (some of us remember how an excise tax on luxury yachts did no favors for blue-collar workers who built toys that float and cost a *lot* of money). All true. But such a person needs to be well-schooled in the fact that it is a baby step from mere conspicuous, ostentatious, unnecessary consumption to fiscal insanity *that harms others*. If you really want it all, and you want it now, the number of people in the entire world who can achieve that without living in the future could be seated at a very small dinner party.

How about, for example, one of the richest families in the world accumulating such a big debt monkey on their backs that they couldn't make mortgage payments? This event, portrayed in the press as a "partial default," launched a European stock-market mini-crisis and threatened worse. Luckily for the debtors, wealthy family members next door came through with a cash infusion. Things then more or less calmed down into what passes for normalcy when people or entities overextend their ambitions and finances in breathtaking amounts. By that kind of normalcy I mean there is one thing we don't know about earthquakes (*when* they will happen) and one thing we do know about earthquakes (they *will* happen).

The previous paragraph describes, of course, the 2009 debt crisis in Dubai. Reopening a line of credit or receiving a truckload of cash from a rich uncle can produce short-term salvation even if it guarantees no long-term results. A few months after its "little" crisis, Dubai continued a tradition of hosting the world's richest day of horse-racing, an event it hosts even though gambling—the source of horse-racing purses—is not allowed in Dubai. Meanwhile, in horse racing half a mile is four furlongs, and one might say the biggest four-furlong wager in history also occurred in Dubai in 2010. After the emirate's "partial default" and Europe's equity nerves had been calmed for the moment, Dubai formally dedicated the world's tallest man-made structure. At 2,717 feet the Burj Khalifa tower actually soars somewhat more than four furlongs. It is aptly named after the ruler of next-door Abu Dhabi, who sent Dubai the $25 billion that prevented a desert fiscal meltdown. That leaves the tower project with "nothing" to be done but find a half-mile-high stack of the world's deepest-pocketed renters, and then amortize the debt. The tower was a mere footnote on Dubai's living-in-the-future shopping list. Stay tuned.

The U.S. Congress and President are a diverse group of elected officials, not a close-knit family of incredibly wealthy oil-and-gas oligarchs. The U.S. House and Senate have not lately built an office tower far into the sky. The United States has, however, sent spacecraft into the neighborhood of Mars, and beyond. I say this not by way of comparing the merit of such projects. Ego and greed can be wed into all sorts of endeavors, including worthy ones. Philanthropy, for example, is a wonderful thing. If someone has millions of spare dollars and decides to finance a new hospital wing it might be a pure act of sainthood. It also might have something to do with ego. Who cares? Nobody cares, as long as the check doesn't bounce. If it does bounce, an act of charity suddenly becomes a reprehensible, egomaniacal act. It's that baby step across the line into fiscal insanity that concerns us here. Even then we wouldn't much care so long as no one but the check-writer gets hurt. Harm others—your own family, an entire workforce, an entire nation, multiple *generations* of an entire nation—and I think we can safely say we are not talking about numbers on a balance sheet. We are talking about ethics and that lately obsolescent word "morals."

I believe each of us no matter our career choice discovers through experience a "moral" path in the workplace. We observe clients, or customers, co-workers, or bosses whose activities leave a little or a lot to be desired in the matter of ethics. These days the clichés for finding the better path all seem to be stated in terms of "doing the right thing," or asking what Jesus—or name a deity or secular "good person" of choice—would do. Sounds to me like what we used to call morals. I regard our country's current balance sheet as a sort of "immoral manifesto"—a declaration that we can make these crippling debts disappear by sending the tab to a future generation. No. That cannot be done. Not without harming people. Grievously so. I regard that to be a crime. The lawyers will tell me there is no such law. There should be, when it comes to the trillions piling up on Uncle Sam's books with no payment in sight. But let's just call it immoral.

How did we get to this immoral place? Why didn't we do the right thing? Most basically, in my view, it goes back to that problem of a mushrooming educational system doing so little educating in basic areas that mean so much. Illiterate backwoodsmen of another era knew the fables and simple pearls of fiscal wisdom emanating from Aesop or Ben Franklin or their own parents. Despite their lack of formal learning, these people *got it*. Their financial world comprised perhaps a few gold coins in a pocket or under a mattress, and some inventory of livestock or logs. In how many families today do you suppose consuming the pizza delivered to the home entertainment center is punctuated by timely warnings to "waste not, want not" or "rather go to bed without dinner than rise in debt"? How many public schools, whose students lack the old tutoring from parents and peers and apprenticeships, teach these things in any meaningful way? I outlined my belief in a K-12 approach to teaching our new-age kids the old truths (in a contemporary context) about money. What I didn't say was that they would also be learning day-to-day application of ethical and moral values. I don't know how one talks about such things to a curriculum committee these days, or whether that is even allowed.

Maybe *The Road Less Traveled* could be used as a text in an upper level of my proposed K-12 curriculum. There you have a book of practical philosophy and morals if there ever was one. When I met M. Scott Peck, and became a close enough friend to call him "Scotty," it was because I had read his signature book and found in it page after page of wisdom I had already confirmed by observation or deduction via my career experiences. So I hit the ground running with Dr. Peck's teachings. No one needed to tell me this was the real stuff. Scotty, however, was a medical doctor, a dynamic speaker, author of a book that sold like nothing the publishing industry had ever seen. *The Road Less Traveled* delivers a message about many things, from spirituality to love to parenting. It reaches *far, far* beyond finances, and Dr. Peck conveyed his message in ways no old numbers guy can. His book spent more than a decade on the New York Times best-seller list, a run that didn't begin until five years after it was published—and what does that tell you about word of mouth?

For a while I gave away *The Road Less Traveled* to colleagues, clients, employees and friends, regarding each copy to be more valuable than a 10-pound bar of gold. I still pass out copies of the Peck book on appropriate occasion, and I know many thousands of people, me included, continue to be enriched by his work. Because of Scotty's untimely death in 2005, I can't say he has endorsed my thoughts here. I can, however, assert that he would have. One of the proudest moments of my life was the day he wrote the *Bankrupt* foreword, in which he said—way back when our national debt was merely appalling: "As a psychiatrist, I am seriously concerned about the health of our nation when it cannot even balance its checkbook—the very beginning of a healing process." He ended the foreword with: "This is a sane book about sanity. Please read it. Perhaps weep, and then scream out in rage about what our leaders are doing to us." Those words were written in late 1992. Dr. Peck's strong encouragement of fiscal sanity back then is one reason I felt obligated to try again with this book.

I think the key to *The Road Less Traveled* and its unprecedented lifespan as a best-seller can be found in one word: "difficult." Not that the book is difficult to read, but that Scott Peck did not candy-coat life's journey, did not pretend there is some easy course to the other side. He proceeded from the fact that life is difficult, that life presents crises, that—and here is the less-traveled path—you are not going to get past those crises without accepting and enduring the pain that comes with genuine solutions. One cannot, in other words and in our context here, sidestep disciplined decisions by grabbing what you want and making unrealistic promises to pay for it in the future. One cannot avoid pain by passing it on to another generation. That is not life, not liberty, not happiness. Especially for the generation where the pain comes to rest.

I have given you a good picture of that recurring moment where I find myself standing on a shop floor—or in a company auditorium, or on a loading dock, or in a shuttered salesroom—giving a workforce the bad news. In *every* case, fiscal reality had become the difficult road for a company to travel. In *every* case, company principals and management had refused to go the difficult route and instead began raiding the future in a futile effort to keep things going as before. In *every* case, all they achieved was to delay and magnify the pain. In the arena of fiscal ethics, these professional situations are a microcosm of what is happening with our government. Whether well-intentioned or corrupt, honest or crooked, any company executive or elected official who tries to sidestep fiscal reality is playing a *greedy* game. And in the end someone else will pay.

It should be no surprise that I had to make another such grim visit during the time I prepared this chapter. Another company was about to go away for good. Perhaps because this book was nearing completion, the scene took on an intense clarity in my mind. I didn't see just the nearly 300 workers who had gathered. I saw—actually envisioned—their absent spouses and children. Such thoughts have occurred to me for decades as I explain to workers that their livelihoods are evaporating. But this day was a stunning experience, as if I were watching a documentary movie about these unfortunate men and women while they watched and listened to me. I imagined the long list of obligations—extended families in need, special health problems, charitable works, kids' educations—that were about to become unfunded. I wondered how anyone could possibly quantify so much pain being unleashed among fewer than 300 people gathered on one shop floor.

And yes, it was actually a shop floor, the deceased entity being a manufacturing company. Its market sector had come under hard times (as all market sectors do, life being difficult for people and companies alike). The company's principals did not respond by bringing appropriate divisions into contact with fiscal reality via cutbacks and new operational budgets. Instead, they took the easy, and to me familiar, path. They exploited and exhausted every dime of debt they could find. The company took its vendors to the limit on payments. Its asset-based line of credit at the bank was maxed out. And, despite being buried in unsold inventory, production lines were kept humming because one lending source remained—the line of credit banks extend based on, yes, inventory. None of the difficult and painful things that should have been done got done. The company's funeral was assured before my phone rang on the case. Forget a turnaround; yet another liquidation was at hand.

The employees did not know this as they reported to work, only that a mandatory meeting would be held. The principals stayed away—not surprisingly a common occurrence. As I and several associates arrived, machines were silent, workers were gathered on the floor with coffee in hand, chatting. It would not be at all accurate to say it was a picnic atmosphere; there was apprehension. I could hear one employee banter as we arrived, "We're in trouble now—the suits are here." But I believe hardly anyone, perhaps no one, anticipated or even considered as a possibility the extent of the bad news to come.

With all the production machinery at a halt, and with everyone growing quiet to hear what I had to say, a lone air compressor ground away off in a corner, an eerie sort of background music to the scene. I explained that, through no fault of their own, the good work they had been doing for years had come to an end. I told them there was not enough business to keep the company going. I said some of them would be called back, briefly, to complete some work in progress (I didn't explain that completed inventory is worth more than scrap, which is what any partially completed job amounts to). I said my usual few words about having seen thousands of people survive such a difficult time and prosper again elsewhere. I said some of the no doubt offensive but absolutely necessary words about gathering up their belongings as they left, while please being sure not to confuse any company property with their own. I wished them well. And McTevia & Associates began its professional task of seeing to it that what was left of this company was protected for its creditors, and liquidated so as to bring them as close to whole as possible. Which, as in many cases, would not be very close.

All through this process, which I have done so many times and will continue to do, I am—by virtue of my experience and skill—one of the best quantifiers around. I can look at inventory and scrap and receivables and unpaid debts and I can click the numbers in my head as quickly and accurately as anyone in this business. That, of course, is what I did on this day as I prepared for my associates to do their work. It's the "movie" of that day, though, that stayed with me. I still see it, in sharp focus. If I saw them on the street, I could identify some of the people standing before me in that documentary.

Without a new commitment to the cornerstone of fiscal ethics—not spending money you don't have and cannot ever hope to have—it is simply impossible for me to avoid seeing the same kind of movie playing out on the widest of screens, stretched from sea to sea. The only good news I can see in this film is that the road to fiscal sanity may be less traveled, and full of pain; but there *is* a road.

8

There's a Way—
But is There a Will?

*After 65 years in which politics in the West
was, mostly, about giving things away to
voters, it's now going to be, mostly, about
taking things away. Goodbye Tooth Fairy
politics, hello Root Canal politics.*

— Thomas L. Friedman, *New York Times*,
May 9, 2010.

*What someone or something is remembered
for or what they have left behind that is
remembered, revered or has impacted current
events and the present day.*

— "Legacy" definition in Wikipedia,
May 9, 2010.

This is the most difficult of chapters; this is the easiest of chapters. Everyone knows what must be done to get us out of this crisis. Anyone who paid attention has known for a very long time. But until recently very few have been willing to admit to the problem, or even talk about it. As of this moment lots of people are talking about it, but very few are willing to do those things everyone knows must be done. That struggle is likely to be the most bitter political process ever seen by any American now alive.

Why? How can it possibly be true that the U.S. government's financial future increasingly heads toward domination by debt service, but we haven't even begun to implement the obvious solution?

Excellent questions. Let me ask two more.

How and why did I take something so obvious (it can be stated in a single sentence) and stretch it into an entire book back in 1992? And why am I stretching it into still another book nearly two decades later?

The way out of financial crisis and the path to fiscal sanity *is* simple and obvious. It is no secret. People and governments—especially governments—nonetheless pay no attention. *Bankrupt* was, and this book is, my part in attempting to contribute whatever additional words, whatever experiences, whatever illustrations... *whatever*... might make our society pay attention and summon the will to act. Individuals (who *do* matter in the big picture) need to pay attention. But even more so, the debt-addicted conglomerate in Washington, D.C., needs to pay attention. This society could weather a tsunami of individual bankruptcies. The bankruptcy of our federal government, however, threatens to take down *all* Americans. It threatens all the attributes and achievements that have made America greater than the sum of its more than 300 million constituent parts. A lack of will to choose the obvious, if difficult, path has put us on the very brink of fiscal self-destruction. Could any policy decision except nuclear warfare be so nonsensically tragic?

The single simple sentence of obvious truth, verifiable throughout the voluminous history of individuals and companies mired in fiscal crisis, is this: There are only three ways out—you can increase revenues or you can decrease expenditures or, as almost certainly will be necessary, you can do both. That sentence is so simple it hurts. It is so obvious that only the guile of a politician or the obfuscation of a Ph.D can tip its truth upside down. Washington's greatest ally in steering away from fiscal sanity is not fact, and not logic. It is pain. Not pain's presence, but contemporary society's boundless capacity for causing greater pain in the future by dodging pain in the present.

In recent years, journalists and commentators have become fond of the phrase "kicking the can down the road." It began to pop up in print and on the air every time government put off making a decision about anything, major or minor. It's a good analogy, however clichéd it may have become. What these commentators need to understand is that the national debt is a can that dwarfs all other cans combined. Eventually debt accumulates bulk and weight that make kicking ever more difficult. This already has happened. Kicking will become not merely more difficult but pain will set in. That is happening right now. And finally, amid excruciating pain, all the kicking in the world will not move this can one inch into the future. At that point the future will be *now*, and it will be desolate—all because we refused to heed fundamental fiscal truth that can be expressed in one sentence.

I don't pretend any ability to predict exactly how many more miles our growing debt load can be kicked down the road. I've been watching for a very long time, though, and it's fascinating to observe—as the debt grows ever more unkickable and the deferred pain ever more unmanageable—how crowded my vantage point is becoming. The simple one-sentence fiscal truth is no truer than it ever was. But the elephant of debt in the living room has gotten so big that more and more people are taking notice. We need more of that. And then still more. But above all we need quick action from our elected officials. If you are religious, I recommend prayer. Congress, after all, knows everything there is to know about avoiding pain. Congress is the one writing checks while kicking all those overdraft notices into the future.

To those Ph.D's and economists and political theorists who see this differently than I do, let me say, yes, I do realize that the U.S. economy is a wondrous, marvelous engine. I do understand that this great engine does not answer *precisely* to the same laws of gravity that define whether a household budget is tethered to reality. I do understand—just as I understand the purpose and value of credit and reasonable debt to a corporation—that the U.S. government and this economy are capable of sustaining a reasonable package of borrowing and other fiscal obligations (assuming, of course, a certain level of economic growth over a certain period of time). But I also understand the abysmally low batting average of economic predictions, and the uncertainties of economic quantification.

Randomly select a jury of 12 experts and sequester them. Ask them not to emerge until they reach a verdict on exactly how "the national debt" should be meaningfully defined, and the precise maximum prudent level the national debt should be allowed to reach as a percentage of our Gross Domestic Product. I highly doubt the 12 experts would reach a verdict even regarding this one basic definition and one basic measurement. Not in my lifetime. It's also possible the United States government will not gorge itself into default, or the equivalent, in my lifetime. But if I had to wager which would come first, the economists' verdict or a U.S. default, my bet would be on default. Or some other very bad-news resolution to Washington's Ponzi scheme.

I do understand—and I think most Americans understand—that the federal government can deploy unique powers of debt resolution not available to any person, company, or lower level of government. None of these resolutions is pleasant. Default never is. Whatever term we use, we are talking about a bloody mauling of this country's once unblemished credit— man's confidence in man. If this day of reckoning arrives the hard way, the federal government will mix and match several means of giving the largest haircut the world ever has seen. Not just creditors here and around the world, but every American will be lined up for shearing. No one can say exactly what this reckoning will look like. But on our current course the hardest of landings is inevitable. Even a course correction to the softest possible landing will take us somewhere between a rock and a hard place.

When its debt scheme finally collapses, one path our federal government can choose is to default, literally and in the traditional manner. Just like a banana republic. The United States has never done this, which is not to say it can't happen. Especially in light of recent fiscal history, current events, and the prevailing mindset as the nation sails into the future. In a default scenario, the Treasury would tell its bond and T-bill owners something like: "Sorry, you won't be getting your money back, let alone interest. But it looks like we can give you 25 cents on the dollar." Unlike a corporate default, a U.S. government default would involve no bankruptcy court, no trustee, no overseer of any kind. The overseer itself would be going into default, setting all its own rules—although I guess the International Monetary Fund and the diplomatic corps would stake claims and lodge protests like the usual swarm of unsecured creditors. Mostly I imagine the world would gasp, loudly, then run off to secure any of its own assets that weren't floating away in our bubbling wake.

Or Washington can simply print enough funny money to pay its obligations. The cheapened dollar would not, of course, fool any longtime Chinese or Japanese or other buyers of Washington's debt (and accumulators of our currency). Nor, for that matter, would the cheapened dollar fool any retiree whose $1,000 Social Security check became, overnight, worth a fraction of its former self at the grocery store. This would, in a way, be the seamless "solution" to the problem. First we pretend debt doesn't matter, then we pretend our debt went away with no consequences.

Or, the federal government can become the champion promise-breaker in all of world history. Unlike T-bills and other equities that would amount to a formal default if not honored, the Congress of the United States has committed itself to spending trillions of dollars on strongly implied or clear and outright promises. Try this. Stack up one pile of federal debt and call it "traditional," meaning cash the Treasury went out and borrowed from lenders. Stack up a second pile and call it "mere promises." At this writing, Washington's stack of mere promises is three times as high as the stack of Treasury borrowing. These mere promises include, of course, payouts under the Social Security and Medicare "entitlement programs" (is anything more clearly a promise than an *entitlement*?). To that stack one can add pension benefits for government workers, and the entire range of benefits and services promised to our military veterans. These and other "mere promises" dwarf the other pile of debt, and will only continue to grow unless new legislation orders a restructuring of these promises. Some will argue that future promises decreed by existing law (and subject to repeal by new law) are not real debits. They would be wrong. Ask any accountant.

Or, Washington can weave a crazy quilt of all the above strategies, subject to whatever political horse trading it might do here and around the world.

In any case, the burgeoning pile of loans to the Treasury can become, all by itself, enough to bump our runaway train off the tracks. Honest and skilled people will tell you this is true. But rather than argue the point, perhaps the best way to understand the peril posed by our "national debt" is to decide whether that stack of "mere promises" should be included. As someone who has been present at the restructuring or liquidation of countless debt-ridden enterprises, I can tell you the answer. *Of course it should be included.* Debt was the fatal weapon in all my professional cases. Any debt. A creditor's refusal to supply raw material, or the lack of cash to pay workers on the shop floor, will be the straw that finally puts a "Closed" sign up on a factory entrance. But it was the crippling level of *all* the company's debt, be it for steel or for executive golf outings or unfunded pension accounts that choked the firm to death. Runaway debt, and a refusal to keep operations trimmed to a level in line with revenues, will sink *any* enterprise. How much greed and arrogance does it take to operate the world's largest enterprise as if it is exempt from gravity's pull?

On any fiscal day of reckoning, certain creditors might receive the most radical haircut possible (they'll be left bald), and certain others will recover varying percentages of what they are owed. Some creditors, in other words, are more equal than others. Not on a balance sheet, however. Expenditures are expenditures. Fiscal obligations are fiscal obligations. Companies are required to tell shareholders, promptly, of all new *future* obligations—such as expenses that will be incurred as a result of new legislation passed by Congress. A balance sheet isn't about which creditor will fare best after a bankruptcy occurs. A balance sheet is about taking a realistic look at a company's fiscal operations and obligations. A properly read and utilized balance sheet is a tool for *avoiding* bankruptcy. If only our elected officials had the ability and/or willingness to read the federal balance sheet.

That is why both good management and common sense demand combining the U.S. government's pile of borrowed-money debt with the much larger pile of "mere promises" to citizens. And that is why the Peter G. Peterson Foundation had it right in mid-2010 when it estimated the "Real National Debt" to be $62.3 trillion. That number is not the rant of some radical zealot. Pete Peterson is a highly successful businessman and former U.S. Secretary of Commerce. His philanthropic activities include a billion-dollar endowment for the foundation, which is devoted to increasing "public awareness of the nature and urgency of key economic challenges threatening America's future." The foundation President is David Walker, former U.S. Comptroller General, a job in which he also was director of the Government Accounting Office.

Naysayers have it right when they assert that the mere promises included in the foundation's "Real National Debt" do not expose government to risk of default as traditionally defined. Of course that is true. The 535 members of Congress could gather tomorrow morning and vote to break every one of those promises (though I don't think that is what the naysayers have in mind). All that promise-breaking would eliminate, in a flash, three-quarters of our Real National Debt. It would also launch civil war in one form or another and the beginning of the end of American society as we know it. So I modestly suggest that these mere promises must indeed be treated as a part of what we are talking about here— our national *debt*.

The $62.3 trillion estimate is an excellent place to start a serious discussion about restructuring and downsizing our government before it bloats itself into collapse. I am speaking, of course, as a turnaround practitioner—hoping our nation will pay attention to its balance sheet in time to be a bona fide restructuring project and not just the bleakest of disaster zones, a sort of fiscal Chernobyl. It seems to me Congress would more likely decree that all future wars must be fought by an Army of 535 elected officials (with the most dangerous missions assigned by seniority) than eliminate a program that has a vote or two attached to it back home. So you understand I'm on the pessimistic side when it comes to Congress acting with the required speed and seriousness of purpose. We face a profound crisis and meantime a clear absence of will among the only 535 people who can solve that crisis. Could we possibly be in a worse spot?

Discussing how to summon that will on behalf of our U.S. Representatives and Senators, and whether that is even possible, means we are entering the home stretch of this book. Again, as in other chapters, I need to say how fascinating it has been to watch events and, mostly, non-events play out while I've put this manuscript together. Here are three such news stories that occurred as this chapter's words made their way onto my computer screen. First, a presidential deficit commission, sworn to be a bipartisan enterprise, held its initial meeting. Second, the 186-member International Monetary Fund warned that even if a global economic recovery takes hold, world economies and governments face a serious threat because of high levels of sovereign debt. Third, America's debt disaster has blossomed, at last, as a topic worthy of mention by news commentators and interviewers who once avoided debt talk as fiercely as they avoid, say, nostalgic discussion of the Eisenhower years. Warnings about the danger lurking in our national debt—which in 1993 generated just two replies from the 536 elected officials to whom I personally distributed a copy of *Bankrupt*—suddenly can be found everywhere. It would be fun to see how many times "unsustainable" has been uttered or written by Washington reporters in the past year as compared to 1993. My rough guess is that use of "unsustainable" has skyrocketed, usually appearing with this book's topic, as in "unsustainable debt."

As rhetoric goes, this stream of verbiage and sudden proclamations of interest in fiscal sanity aims in the right direction. No quarrel there. But let's not forget that even as our politicians give lip service to fiscal sanity they also step forward to advocate unfunded programs that will *add to the nation's debt*. My professional career won't let me regard all this talk as "*a step* in the right direction." Talk is not a step, it is talk. Action is a step. I need to see some kind of tangible implementation of the one-sentence, three-pronged, immutable truth about how to achieve fiscal sanity. Then I'll concede we are seeing movement, even if at a glacial and meaningless pace.

Consider the bipartisan deficit panel created by President Obama's executive order. Who could possibly object? But remember, the executive order was issued for one reason: Congress refused to form such a panel on its own. And any proposals that might emerge from the presidential panel's effort will be meaningless unless approved by... Congress. How's that for a prospectus? Want to buy a few shares in that venture? I'm sure the news media will continue to call this panel "The Deficit Commission." That fits. Its stated goal is not to find ways of reducing the debt—and interest on it—but to reduce annual deficits to three percent. We really need to address that debt, not just the deficit. To say nothing of all those "mere promises." The President's bureaucratic name for the panel actually has it exactly right. It's the National Commission on Fiscal Responsibility and Reform. Perfect. We need fiscal responsibility. We need reform. Go for it, fellas. Once again, if you have religious belief, prayer would be appropriate.

Nothing in America's current hyper-partisan political life suggests this commission will succeed in its mission. Everything in my half-century of observing human nature amid fiscal disaster suggests Congress will kick this can the last possible inch down the road. I would consider it a blessing if events prove my prediction woefully wrong. I make these negative observations not to waste your time or mine in tossing a wet blanket on whatever spark of progress toward fiscal sanity *might* be afoot. My viewpoint is meant to be taken as an experienced practitioner's warning. *Longstanding* warning. A lot of positive things can happen when negatives are addressed rather than ignored.

Such is the spirit in which I tell you what I fully expect our elected leaders will do. That is, the same thing owners and managers of debt-ridden and doomed companies do, rather than getting straight to the necessary task of restructuring their operations. Having taken their companies to the brink by borrowing instead of operating realistically, they try to *borrow* themselves out of their crisis. Invariably. And onward for whatever overleveraged distance into infinity they are allowed to travel. You would be amazed at how far that scheme can be carried, even in the private sector. The last bit of collateral is pledged for a bigger line of credit at the bank. Vendor payments are delayed for 90, then 120 days, then longer. Internal accounts that still have a positive balance are raided. Legal boundaries perhaps get crossed, such as not funding employee retirement accounts. None of the creditors wants to see a customer go away, so the creditors become enablers for a time, thus magnifying their own losses. By the time someone like me is summoned, the company's finances resemble an engine that has been so far run past the red line that its internal parts have melted.

Smart people do this to companies. Good people do this to companies. It logically follows that in a the era of paying for a Happy Meal with a credit card, people smart enough and good enough to serve in Congress can do it to an entire country. It is an institutional version of Queen's rock anthem about wanting it all, and wanting it now. In the case of Congress it gets more devious, the institutionalized deceit gets more massive. It becomes not just about trying to get it all, but getting it all for nothing by passing the tab on—as only Congress can do—to another generation. It is about an entity, Congress, that does not have a vigilant banker and a creditors' committee and a bankruptcy court waiting to pounce on living-in-the-future schemes. It is about the ability to borrow money when any other institution would be shut down as insolvent. It is about the politicization of debt, something that is inevitable when even a seemingly bottomless access to credit reaches toxic levels.

What is the politicization of debt? Intentionally sinking the value of a currency would be an example. Some would say refusing to recognize that our debt includes a pile of "mere trillion-dollar promises written into the law" is an example of politicization. Trying to *talk* our financial obligations into something of no consequence would definitely be an example of politicizing the national debt. You will see endless barrels of ink and hours of air time politicizing the simple one-sentence summation of fiscal sanity after the National Commission on Fiscal Responsibility and Reform sends its recommendations to Congress. Assuming, of course, the commission is able to come up with a unified report rather than a split decision like a bad boxing match. I wish them well.

The fact is, it is time, right now, to accept pain. There is a lot of pain to accept. But less pain now than a year from now, which will be less pain than a year from then, and on into a future like a devilish sort of compound interest. For the moment, an element of choice remains. Not a lot of choices, and all of them difficult. But at this moment there is still opportunity for an orderly attempt at restructuring, for stopping the flow of bad checks, for getting our national balance sheet to acknowledge what works and what doesn't work, what the people want and what the people don't want. It is far past time to analyze the new demographics of America, and how government will deal with the fact that retirees live many years longer than they used to, and that meanwhile the number of Americans in the workplace is decreasing. And more. We need to do these things. That is obvious. If you think General Motors was allowed to evolve into something that made no sense and didn't work, I invite you to take a closer look at GM's new majority owner. The American automakers' avoidance of pain and restructuring was nothing when compared to the debt-buried conglomerate headquartered in Washington, D.C.

We Americans will have our disagreements about how to reintroduce fiscal sanity to our government, how to distribute the pain across this generation and future generations. But how can *anyone* at this late date deny it needs to be done? I have told you more than once that troubled companies deny this need right up to the day I must stand on their shop floor, say it's all over, and send everyone home. But this biggest of all "companies" is all of us—including Americans not yet born. We are talking about a *legacy* of bankruptcy. The moral equivalent of sending all of us home should not be an option, and I wish I didn't even have to say I think our leaders and our culture are capable of taking us there.

I have a few more things to say about the *way* to approach these things, and about what might happen if we insist on kicking the can until it will not budge that final inch into the future. But seeing how and why to pull our government's finances back from the insane future to the sane present is very easy compared to finding the *will* needed make it happen. Especially when all the power to act lies with just 535 elected officials who led us to where we are.

I have tried to share a window into my experience with debt crises. I think you can now see why my background screams out that nothing meaningful is going to happen until Congress can no longer borrow a single dollar. Most Americans probably would find such a prediction shocking and not credible. But anyone who reads these pages will understand that this "shocking and not credible" behavior is exactly what I have been looking at in *all* my cases for many decades. If this book then helps someone convince even a handful of those 535 why they need to act, and how serious their actions must be, that is good. If one or two of the 535 themselves actually read this book, that is also good—no matter how angry it makes them.

One last thought about summoning the will to act. If you think you recognized a familiar wise saying paraphrased and paraphrased again on these pages, you are correct. I have shared it hundreds of times with clients who were finally attending their fiscal day of reckoning. Not one of them has seen fit to disagree. The saying is: "Today is the Tomorrow you worried about Yesterday."

9

Is Washington Too Big to Fail? No.

"The longer we wait the more severe, the more draconian, the more difficult the adjustments are going to be."

— Federal Reserve Chairman Ben Bernanke in January 2010, warning the Senate Budget Committee that the United States must act quickly to reduce exploding costs of entitlement programs.

And so it comes full circle. You'll recall that when I was a young man helping invent a profession that restructures enterprises brought down by unsustainable debt, my line of work didn't yet have a name. That's why I carried a business card announcing myself as an adjustment consultant. Back in that more fiscally sane era I didn't imagine the United States government one day marching headlong into insolvency. I certainly didn't foresee the irony, from my perspective, of the Federal Reserve chairman warning of "difficult" adjustments lying ahead. That is, of course, precisely what I warned when I wrote *Bankrupt* in 1992 and what I am warning here. Unlike Ben Bernanke, I am not understating or sugarcoating the message, especially at this late date. "Difficult" doesn't begin to describe the pain that waits at the end of the line. "Adjustment" sounds more like a quick visit to a chiropractor than the major fiscal restructuring this country requires. Such action is needed immediately—which is what Ben Bernanke, ever so gently, told those senators. "Immediately," however, is a pipe dream when it comes to fiscal sanity in Washington. Too bad for us.

Exactly five months after Bernanke gave the testimony quoted above, Paul Volcker—the widely respected dean of American economists and financial-policy advisers—said time is "growing short" for solving our deficit and entitlement problems. "Today's concerns may soon become tomorrow's existential crises," Volcker said. Chapter Eight explained my profound doubt that our elected leaders will act before the mother of all debt-driven train wrecks performs an involuntary and cataclysmic "adjustment." Is that what Paul Volcker expressed nervousness about, 18 years after *Bankrupt* was published and mere days before this book went to the printer? Sounds like it to me, if I understand what "existential crisis" means. Sounds like Niall Ferguson warning about "the fatal arithmetic of imperial decline" unless we undertake radical fiscal reform. Sounds like Pat Buchanan warning: "What the looming fiscal crisis of this country portends is nothing less than a test of whether this democratic republic is sustainable."

As more and more citizens realize a day of fiscal reckoning has become unavoidable, most might find it incredible that our elected leaders remain not so much like deer frozen in headlights as like ostriches with heads buried in red ink. This despite being handed so much sane fiscal advice from a chorus that keeps growing in numbers and volume. I don't find the lack of congressional action incredible. I find it totally expectable. I have to believe that Doug Elmendorf, the Congressional Budget Office director, understood the tongue-in-cheek dark humor of his words when he testified: "I think most observers expect that the government will act; that the unsustainability will be resolved through action, not through witnessing some collapse down the road." I for one believe that however and whenever Congress acts, it will not remotely resemble anything timely and meaningful, and I think you understand why I see it that way. But let's press on and use this chapter to discuss what must be done, whether or not Congress summons the will to do it. It won't take long for you to see why our government keeps performing like so many ostriches. It's one thing to stand on a shop floor and say, as I have so many times: "I'm sorry I have to bring you such painful, life-changing news." It's another thing altogether to deliver that same message to an entire nation, and have to add: "It's all my fault." That's one reason the warnings and the obvious fiscal truths will continue to be ignored, and our ticking debt bomb will be kicked on down the road.

One thing I am not going to do here is try to assemble a detailed and definitive digest of all the numbers and projections illustrating why action is necessary. That is, as Bill Cosby said, like debating the question: "Why is there air?" Common sense and more importantly a career as a first-responder to debt disasters led me to write a book-length warning nearly two decades ago on behalf of future generations. Now, as I put this volume to bed, Iceland's bankruptcy looks like the canary in the coal mine, a tiny nation gone belly up while Greece gasps for air and most of Europe is coughing badly. Who knows precisely where Europe's own debt-driven mess will lead, and exactly when it will get there? Not me, for sure. But I do know, better than anyone on your speed dial, exactly what must be done when debt reaches unsustainable, suffocating levels. What's needed, always, is a genuine restructuring. Live within your means or die, if it isn't already too late. The greater the debt burden and the further the enterprise has strayed from fiscal reality, the deeper the restructuring, the greater the pain, the less likelihood of success. This is not economic theory. This is fiscal fact.

True, you can find the odd Nobel-winning economist writing newspaper columns headlined "Greece doesn't matter," and claiming that warnings about our debt disaster amount to fear-mongering. I'm not going to reach deep into "Why is there air?" to wage that battle. It's not my specialty and I'm not going there, for two reasons.

First, countless highly credentialed non-political or centrist sources have analyzed the economic impact of our debt insanity in ways that would convert almost anyone to the cause of sanity. You needn't depend on me for that kind of detail. The internet provides easy access, for example, to the Peter G. Peterson Foundation's extremely sane arithmetic regarding traditional debt plus all those "mere promises" such as Social Security and Medicare. The Concord Coalition is devoted to an attempt at making Washington understand that at least a modest tip of the hat to reality would be a good thing. Both groups' web sites take you straight to pertinent and timely data. The columns written by Robert Samuelson in Newsweek and the Washington Post have repeatedly addressed related issues, especially demographics and entitlements, in serious but readable fashion. One can find testimony even from the Congressional Budget Office (yes, that Congress) assuring we will encounter a crushing tsunami of debt and broken promises if Congress does not act. Non-partisan sources abound illustrating what will happen with all this debt and all these obligations if no action is taken (utter disaster), and what will happen meanwhile (something worse than utter disaster) if the cost of debt service rises significantly, which it will. These facts are out there in plain sight, like the Emperor's New Clothes. The internet will keep the numbers crunched and up-to-date for you. I do personally promise you this: The national debt, however you choose to define it and measure it, will not decrease 10 cents between the time this paragraph is typed and the time you read it.

Second, I think this book offers a unique perspective amid all the economic and political experts who will be paraded before you almost daily for many months and no doubt years to come. If any senator or talk-show host or columnist has made even two or three "sorry, but it's all over for you" speeches on a factory floor or sales floor, I'm not aware of it. If any pundit is well-practiced in glancing at a balance sheet and accurately foreseeing an enterprise's future solvency (or lack thereof) as easily as you can back out of your garage without using GPS, I am not aware of it. If you will be hearing from any other analyst or observer of any kind who has spent half a century overseeing days of reckoning invariably caused by unrealistic levels of debt, I'm not aware of it. If any of the 535 people who need to step up and restructure the fiscal life of Earth's most economically powerful country has successfully restructured so much as a three-store shoe-retailing chain, I am not aware of it. So instead of contributing to a debate about "Why is there air?"...let me give you my basic thoughts about restructuring U.S.A. Inc.

It has to begin with getting real about the depth of the problem. As you know, communicating reality to clients always has been an unwritten part of my job description. When I am called to the scene of a debt disaster long after it's too late, even then the client—or the person or entity to whom I have been dispatched by their creditors or a court—denies a problem exists. What form does this denial take? That's right—after being pulled to the bottom of the pond by the dead weight of runaway debt, and while sucking water into their lungs, the principals greet me with a request that I help them borrow still more money. How's that for an insanely vicious circle? I have developed skills in convincing most business principals and managers that their train has in fact stopped, and no, it's no longer on the tracks, and yes, that stuff all around them is wreckage, and no, they cannot borrow money to print more tickets for sale to passengers who want a ride to Schenectady.

U.S.A. Inc. is hardly an ordinary client, though. I imagine those ice carts mentioned in the Prologue are still pushed each day from congressional office to congressional office, just as they were when I visited Capitol Hill in 1993. If so, it can't be said that I have developed skills in convincing our elected officials of fiscal facts I successfully convey almost every day in the private sector. Nor has anyone else—whether the ice carts still roll down the halls, or not. Why do those ice carts fascinate me so much? Because it's such a struggle in the halls of Congress to find even a symbolic seriousness of purpose and willingness to do the difficult and unpopular to halt our debt disaster. That is what restructuring is all about. Congress, I am certain, will instead find ways of borrowing itself even deeper into the mud at the bottom of the pond than it already has. So that first step toward restructuring U.S.A. Inc.—getting the principals to wake up and smell the reality—will have to be done by someone else. Maybe you and other citizens, maybe on an election day, can get the message across.

Let me say one more word—literally one more word—about how deep our culture of debt has led this society into spending money it doesn't have, all day every day. It's a handy word that seems to fit insolvent governments and government agencies at every level. By the time you read these pages this word might be used in so many headlines, and on so many talk shows, that it will be declared illegal. The word is "draconian." Living beyond your means for years on end always demands a draconian solution. No other kind of solution will do. Keep in mind that, unlike the state and local entities in the following headlines, our federal government has the power to ignore reality so far into the future that a new word will have to be invented for Washington's day of reckoning. As the fourth headline shows, California—with an economy larger than most countries—already is seeking such a word.

Officials react to 'draconian' cuts
—NorthJersey.com headline on school budgets.

Cuts to Idaho educators draconian, unnecessary
—Headline on *Idaho Post-Tribune* web site
atop post from a teacher's spouse.

Draconian budget cuts loom, governors say
—*USA Today* headline.

California faces budget cuts 'beyond draconian'
—*Christian Science Monitor* headline.

Draco, by the way, was a Greek lawgiver who lived several centuries before the birth of Christ. Legend has it that when complaints arose about applying the death penalty for relatively minor offenses, Draco responded that the penalty was appropriate—he just couldn't come up with a more severe punishment for more severe crimes. That is why, centuries later, headline writers pull out the word "draconian" to describe any legislation or policy perceived to be harsh. So get ready down at the state and local level for a continuing parade of program cuts that most Americans will regard as draconian—or "beyond." Exactly what else would you expect in a society that starts living on its credit cards, ships its manufacturing base overseas, shifts the bulk of "secure" and pensioned jobs to the government sector, and extends lifespans until retirees outnumber workers?

All the above headlines came from jurisdictions our 535 U.S. Representatives and Senators would call "back home." None of the grim news resulted from federal budget slashing. Whenever circumstances finally force Washington to touch base with fiscal reality, perhaps after everyone has learned how to count past a trillion without blinking, those back-home "draconian" cuts will look like child's play. A local paving project canceled or a couple teachers laid off at your child's grade school? How about cutbacks in a landscape where credit-card receipts keep piling up to pay for two wars and for multi-billion-dollar expenditures almost no one understands or even notices—such as propping up Fannie Mae and Freddie Mac? Federal red ink gushes like the output of a severed artery, and the only response we hear from the spenders is the same thing I hear from doomed businesses: "Let's go borrow more money!"

Unlike those doomed insolvent businesses, the congressional Ponzi scheme is on course to last until a new generation discovers it is reporting to work each day in large part to pay China and Japan interest on all that debt. How much irony can you handle while pretending to laugh? Try this. On the very day this paragraph was written, the U.S. Senate approved a "financial reform act" to be imposed on others.

I guess paragraphs like the above officially make me one of those "deficit hawks" I keep reading about, someone whom apologists for living in the future regard as a stodgy naysayer. I cheerfully accept the deficit hawk label, though I would prefer "reality hawk." I want my descendants free to fly, not weighted to Earth by the greed and fiscal arrogance of earlier generations. It's not an unreasonable wish. Look back to the header atop this chapter. Even Ben Bernanke agrees. He even used the "d" word. Lots of people these days say the right thing when it comes to living in the future. Why is it so difficult to get this message translated into action? That's only a rhetorical question.

You already know the two reasons I don't expect I'll live to see Congress do anything but kick its debt disaster as far down the road as possible. Unlike the businesses I restructure or liquidate, U.S.A. Inc. can (a) obtain seemingly endless loans to support its red ink, and (b) print money. You also know that trying to live in the future by following those two paths is a Ponzi scheme. Literally and beyond all doubt. The federal debt and the federal promises get piled so high that only an unbroken string of perfect or at least tolerable fiscal weather will keep the scam going. We've already reached that point, or so near it (say "retiring Boomers") that it's not worth an argument. When a perfect fiscal storm hits this toxic pile—kaboom! It will be like all of Iceland's SUVs and volcanoes blowing up simultaneously, with a Greek general strike and a nuclear device thrown in for good measure.

Let the experts predict which combination of soaring interest rates, or sudden international distaste for T-bills, or political upheaval somewhere on the globe, or loss of fossil fuel supply for whatever reason, or unforeseen genuine domestic demand upon our resources, or chain of currency collapses...will be the first levee to fail. What matters is we know the perfect storm will arrive, as surely as we knew New Orleans's vulnerability before Katrina hit. And what does Congress have in mind for the day a Category Five fiscal event finally plows into its pile of debt? A FEMA trailer, two years' worth of fast-food coupons, and a daily ice water delivery "just like we have in Congress" for every American? George W. Bush's praise for his FEMA chief—"Brownie, you're doing a heck of a job"—will look absolutely brilliant, and trivial, by comparison with whatever Capitol Hill has to say after the Big One wallops a $13-trillion stack of I.O.U.'s. To say nothing of the much bigger pile of "mere promises" Congress has made to the American people.

When the founders put our national checkbook in the hands of Congress, they could not foresee our current culture of debt. Not the breathtaking scope of it. They could not imagine the generational theft of using their grandchildren's credit card to go to Mars or Afghanistan. I think it's safe for even a non-historian to say our founders would not have favored creating entitlement programs that during one lifetime would soar from zero percent of federal spending to half the budget and still counting. Surely our founders would weep in disbelief and dismay if they knew debt service had become a significant portion of federal spending, with strong likelihood of mushrooming upward. Our capital city is named after a man who warned against trying to live in the fiscal future. How arrogant, in that light, can a government be? This would be merely an issue for political debate if it weren't true that entitlements—and general mismanagement of the federal checkbook—are on course to bankrupt us all. In that case it won't just be money we are talking about. All the intangibles that made Main Street America prosperous and secure and the world's destination of choice will be headed down the toilet along with our grandchildren's prospects. The federal government, whose main job is supposed to be keeping us secure, will have all by itself taken away our security.

Use whichever terminology you wish to describe what needs to be done with U.S.A. Inc.'s balance sheet. Restructuring. Turnaround. Downsizing. Adjustment. Calibration with fiscal reality. However you say it, nearly everybody understands, knows, admits, stipulates, agrees, avows that our nation's fiscal course is unsustainable. They don't hint, wink and nudge, or grudgingly agree. They look you

in the eye and use the word as if they mean it—
"unsustainable." Nearly everybody. The President
of the United States. The chairman of the Federal
Reserve. Probably a majority of the very same 535
officeholders who write all those rubber checks.
They all agree that on some date, one that is coming
at us faster and faster, our current debt trajectory
will burst through the levees of denial. Everyone in
Washington says this, that is, until someone like
Jim Bunning stands up and—for whatever reason,
be it noble or political or merely an old man making
inappropriate sounds in public—takes them at
their word. "Hey," the naysayer asks, "didn't we
agree to pay as we go?" Suddenly, unsustainable
gets redefined as sustainable. Suddenly, the Corps
of Electioneers pronounces the levees to be in good
shape. The rubber checks keep flowing. A few new
programs are even created so more rubber checks
can be written.

Someone has to take the first step of restructuring,
the initial act that follows the admission of a problem.
("I am U.S.A. Inc., and I am a debtaholic.") Someone
has to take away that checkbook. America needs to
take some time off from spending and get back in
touch with basic realities like fully understanding,
at last, how many checks already have been
written—and how many more have been promised.
If a majority in this democracy says none of this
matters—that we ought to just keep bouncing checks
until our money plunges in value, the streets seem
meaner each day, and the Grand Canyon becomes
a Chinese theme park—well, OK. I guess we would

have to live with that, one way or another. Somehow I don't think Americans want to travel that path. If you think my imagery is a bit extreme, fine. Go ask President Obama, Ben Bernanke, Paul Volcker, and several hundred fiscal cowards in Congress to state what they see as the worst-case scenario. What do they think will happen if we try to sustain this debt-ridden path even they call "unsustainable"? What do they mean? In plain English? Take away my tongue-in-cheek Grand Canyon business plan and there is nothing at all surprising about my scenario. Just as there was nothing surprising about what would happen if you put New Orleans under water. It is human nature, I guess, to find an endless supply of disbelief after an impending catastrophe renders its obvious and predictable consequences.

Is Washington too big to fail? My chapter title says "no"—and isn't that phrase, "too big to fail," an interesting double-edged blade? Nothing of course is too big to fail. That's what I meant when I answered "no." The bigger they are, the harder they fall and all that. It is argued these days that the entire planet is failing because one species insists on burning the planet's carbon. How arrogant is it to believe that, but not believe that writing trillion-dollar rubber checks will bankrupt what's left of our economy? This is all very interesting, but it's not what those who ask the too-big-to-fail question mean, whether they speak of Lehman Brothers or U.S.A. Inc. They mean, "Is this thing too big for us to let it fail? Do we need to step in and save it because it is too important to watch it go down the sewer?" In that sense, of course

Washington is too big to fail. America is too important to watch it go down the sewer. But guess what? No one is standing by to bail out Washington. No one is big enough to bail out U.S.A. Inc. Washington has to bail itself out. It needs to restructure, and step one is all about that checkbook.

Fear-mongering? If so, we need a lot more of it. Facts can indeed be fearsome, and fearsome facts can help breed fiscal sanity. Aesop's fiscally sane ant, for example, was a lot more fearful of the coming winter than Aesop's fiscally insane grasshopper. Score one for fear-mongering. It is doubly meaningless, isn't it, for our leaders to tell us our fiscal path is unsustainable but (a) refuse to tell us, forcefully and compellingly, what will happen if we don't change course, and then (b) lead us farther along that unsustainable route? Policy discussion, for example, would be well-served if all citizens understood that workers foot the bill for retirees' health care and Social Security benefits, and that we're spiraling downward toward a 2-to-1 ratio of workers to retirees (from more than 40-to-1 in 1945). That's not even an "if." It is a scheduled event. The ratio is projected to be a hair below 2-to-1 when babies born this year reach age 65. The average combined annual cost of Social Security and Medicare per recipient is now well north of $20,000 and rising. Almost all long-term growth in federal spending is slated to go for Social Security, Medicare, Medicaid, and interest on the federal debt. Those are scary numbers, but one man's fear-mongering is another man's salient fact.

Entitlements aren't called the "third rail" of

American politics for nothing. It is no accident that even a suggestion of raising the age of Social Security eligibility or otherwise tinkering with a broken system gets shoved into a congressional cold locker without discussion and sporting a "dead on arrival" toe tag. One thing about broken programs, cost-inefficient policies, and crippling deficits—despite their pressing need for repair, all of them buy votes back home. In the end, members of Congress not only avoid touching that third rail...they avoid even talking about it in any sense that matters. So, yes, of all the federal budget problems one might talk about, Social Security and Medicare rank right at the top. And right there, in plain sight, nothing happens. Let me put it this way. The destructive use of fear in budgetary matters doesn't lie in talking about nasty consequences of red ink, but in *not* talking about it. Especially when, unlike in the private sector, debt denial can run rampant for several generations. Maybe longer; we're working on that.

In the private sector insolvent companies get restructured (or liquidated). In state and local government, outside overseers are assigned to restructure broken school districts, and trustees sometimes are even appointed to manage bankrupt cities. Nothing but the ballot box, however, stands in the way of fiscal insanity in Washington. As creditors' committees go, the ballot mechanism has not been efficient. Maybe that will change, as the public lately has shown much more interest in deficits and the debt than the people who write the rubber checks. Debt restructuring via ballot box would be good, but one very big question is: When? There is, after all, a due date on this impending catastrophe, even if we don't know exactly what that date may be.

When I say somebody needs to take away the congressional checkbook, I do realize I am advocating something that will never happen and would be (correctly) declared unconstitutional if it did. So why bother to make the point? I suppose because even if it can't happen, something equivalent must happen. Somehow, a tourniquet must be applied to that checking account. For an old turnaround guy, standing on the sidelines and watching the blood flow from nothing more important than a once-honorable corporation is a painful thing. Standing on the sidelines and watching my country bleed out is indescribably horrible.

From my point of view, of course, it would be a fine thing if the Constitution did allow appointment of a bankruptcy trustee for U.S.A. Inc. He would be fully empowered to reel our government back to living within its means, and would be tasked to assure Washington did nothing to imperil future generations' prosperity. I wouldn't want the job myself, because whoever successfully completed such a task would have to live his or her remaining years in the Cheyenne Mountain bunker outside Colorado Springs, or maybe in the federal witness protection program. The job would need a different title, of course. Something less inflammatory. Office of the Debt Czar might do the trick. Except for the "Debt" part, czar is a very popular job description these days.

How would a Debt Czar proceed? You already

know the drill. No matter how elegant the terminology, no matter how many pages in the proposal, no matter how fancy the printed document or the power point graphics, no matter how long the consultant's list of references, in a financial crisis only three things can be done. You need to increase revenues, or decrease expenditures, or—almost always—both. This mother of all restructurings will of course require both. Lots of both.

On the revenue side, U.S.A. Inc. at first glance is a turnaround manager's dream. In the private sector, one cannot simply tell a foundering plastics company's treasurer to put letters in the mail ordering everyone in a 100-mile radius to send money. U.S.A. Inc. can, in a fashion, do exactly that. Unfortunately, that first glance only lasts for half a second. The federal government is empowered to tax, and then tax some more, but there are limits. Several kinds of limits, in fact. The one that matters most to Congress—political limitations on tax hikes from the right, and political limitations from the left regarding who gets taxed—is the least important in the real world. The Debt Czar isn't looking for votes, he's looking for solvency.

But politics aside, there are genuine levels at which soak-the-rich tax schemes become counterproductive, for numerous reasons. Without spending 100 or 1,000 pages pursuing specifics here, let me just refer you to the mountain of research available on that topic. Consult a bundle of sources, toss out the half-dozen that lean most to the right and the half-dozen that lean most to the left, and accept a consensus of what remains. You'll be close enough to the truth. You'll see how rhetoric from both sides about "small business being the source of most job creation" means it's best not to soak people who are not truly rich but just seriously affluent, because they tend to be those job creators. You'll see that when it comes to soaking the truly wealthy it would take an army of IRS staffers rewriting the Tax Code to outsmart their tax attorneys, a costly battle the IRS is destined to lose. So up at the two levels that already are paying the lion's share of income tax there is room, in time of crisis, to impose more. Not enough room, though, to make a major dent in the problem. In other words, use due diligence to collect a reasonable revenue increase, but don't expect to solve your problem that way. (If I were the Debt Czar I would dump the Tax Code altogether and start over with a flat tax or a value added tax or almost anything other than what we have. But I am not going to be the Debt Czar, so I digress.)

Discovering that the higher-hanging fruit isn't going to provide much revenue relative to need, the Debt Czar would move on and order some new taxation on the middle class. That's a tax target usually avoided by politicians because even a shrinking middle class accounts for millions of votes. The Debt Czar would find some significant revenue here, but—and here is the most important "but" in the entire Debt Czar kingdom—getting U.S.A. Inc.'s balance sheet within even shouting distance of equilibrium must overwhelmingly be achieved not by increasing revenues but by decreasing expenditures. Both are necessary, but draconian tax hikes and even tax hikes "beyond draconian" would not approach solving the problem. Remember, we are talking about a current deficit headed toward most of $2 trillion, a traditionally scored debt that's headed next for $14 trillion, and a bunch of "mere promises" that the former comptroller of the United States includes as part of a "real national debt" adding up to $62 trillion (or $200,000 for each American citizen). And you thought your car payment was a burden. Additionally, you may go round up your budget projections of choice and choose to believe, or not believe, Congress's spin on the future cost of its shopping list and its promises. You may make your own decision as to whether it would be wise to have some liquidity to cover future non-fiscal catastrophes. You may guess what must be budgeted for debt service, already a major item, if interest rates rise.

Furthermore, if you want to keep U.S.A. Inc. a going concern, you may find yourself considering establishment of a major and generalized "contingency" budget item. I say this because—and this will be a very long sentence—we live, after all, in a nation where many billions of dollars worth of infrastructure needs have not been met, where state governments are going bankrupt partly because Washington has tried to hand off the cost of various federal promises, where several million jobs have disappeared and are not reappearing, where despite almost a year of tumult about health-care reform there is no real sign that soaring health-care costs will be returning toward Earth any time soon, where many 40-something parents try to cobble a livelihood out of three different fast-food jobs with no benefits while others knock down three times as much income via pensions from government jobs. Feel free to add your own reasons for thinking the revenue projections of future budgets could be written a little more conservatively, and the expenditure side could use a dollar or two in an honest contingency fund instead of pretending emergency expenditures are not really expenditures. I leave it to the Debt Czar's numbers crunchers to come up with specific dollar amounts. But I do know how to read a balance sheet, and if you want an honest accounting, what you see above are some important items for the Debt Czar—and all of us—to think about.

This next item should be no surprise: If I were Debt Czar, I would move this country into the land of balanced budgets. I'd do this for several reasons. I would argue with economists who scoff and say growth will take care of a little deficit spending here and there. I scoff at their scoffing. Predicting growth is a fascinating and feel-good enterprise, kind of like predicting every generation will live better than every previous generation, or houses will always be worth more tomorrow than they are today. That kind of cocksure optimism is so American, and so unlike the real world. Besides, we are not talking about a real corporation where, if management chooses, it can impose real budgets. We are talking about U.S.A. Inc.—and how would you like to buy yourself a new fighter plane or new Bridge to Somewhere that actually cost what Congress budgeted it to cost? Also don't forget we are sailing on those uncharted waters where manufacturing jobs have disappeared like yesterday's rainbow, the service economy seems like ancient history, the IT economy seems like someone on the phone from Mumbai answering your computer service question, and the loss of jobs during the current Great Recession doesn't look like a passing phenomenon. A good month has been redefined lately as a month where barely enough new jobs have been created to match population growth—and it has taken government-sector jobs to accomplish that much. So I like balanced budgets in the real world where I work, and I like balanced budgets at least as much when I think about the insolvent U.S.A. Inc.

Nonetheless, despite my opinion that we ought to balance the budget right now (and start paying down the debt), let's imagine our hypothetical Budget Czar has not been ordered to balance the budget at all. Let's say he has been told to reduce the federal deficit to a "mere" three percent of GDP. It's not a number pulled from the clouds. That is exactly the blueprint the White House ordered its Deficit Commission to return with by early 2011. I believe this charter sets the bar so low as to mean almost nothing, except perhaps kicking the deficit bomb further into the future. Even though economic theory and the sprawling federal government are not my bailiwick, it seems obvious to me that honest emergency spending and not-so-honest cost overruns (not just for fighter planes, but for much bigger items such as health-care reform) will, by themselves, make any "three percent" budget deficit into a wishful joke at the end of the day. That's without admitting the peril in trying to predict the cost of borrowing money, no small matter when you are talking about the world's largest borrower— which has to borrow to service debt it already has incurred. But, as I said, here we are imagining that our Budget Czar is tasked to do nothing beyond the goals set for President Obama's Deficit Commission. Guess what—and here I go being negative again—it won't, in my opinion, happen. That is to say, the Debt Czar could make it happen. The Debt Commission won't. In my opinion. Which is why we are doing this mind exercise of appointing a Debt Czar.

We can't tax our way out of this debt disaster. We have to increase revenues, but we also have to make big-time, serious cuts on the expenditure side of the balance sheet. Everybody knows this. The Peterson Foundation recently conducted a remarkable survey of senior economic officials from the last eight administrations, all the way back through Lyndon Johnson's "Great Society" tenure. The survey included Treasury secretaries, Fed chairmen, Congressional Budget Office directors, heads of the Council of Economic Advisers, and ranking members of House and Senate Budget and Ways and Means committees. That's 30 years' worth of top economic policymakers from both political parties. Here are some amazing results— not that it's amazing these people agree on these matters, but that it's amazing so many people can understand fiscal truth and yet nothing gets done:

- One hundred percent of both Republican and Democratic officials surveyed said the federal government "is on an unsustainable long-term fiscal path."

- More than 90 percent of officials from both parties said that if we don't move quickly to repair our long-term commitment to red ink, we will plunge into "another major economic crisis."

- Majorities of these former highly placed economic policy officials in both parties said failure to act will "crowd out other important public investments" and "cause a significant rise in interest rates" and cause "an eventual decline in Americans' standard of living."

- More than two-thirds of Republican and Democratic administrations said that both an increase in revenues and a decrease in expenditures would be necessary (does that sound familiar?).

Many of us foresee even worse consequences from our spiraling debt. But what you see above is nonetheless a broad consensus, from left and right and from administrations including LBJ's and Ronald Reagan's, that we are sailing into bad news because of our debt addiction and we need to cut back spending. I don't lightly call this a "remarkable" survey. Even more remarkable is that our elected officials, meanwhile, are totally uninterested in doing anything. Don't forget, Congress refused even to appoint a commission to talk about this subject, which is why the Deficit Commission was created by the White House. Sad translation and prediction: The Deficit Commission's main function will turn out to be that familiar Washington role—kicking our debt bomb into the future and hoping for the best. I admit I might be wrong. I certainly hope I am wrong. But even if Alan Simpson and Erskine Bowles and the other 16 commissioners emerge from behind closed doors with unanimous approval of a coherent proposal, what happens next? Keep in mind there is no way even a low-bar and phony three percent budget deficit can be achieved without adjustments in entitlement programs. And all a commission can do is recommend such adjustments. Only Congress, which refuses even to talk about doing it, can do it. As I said, good luck fellas. That is why mind exercises about restructuring U.S.A. Inc. with a Debt Czar are not an entirely useless thing. Some problems don't require thinking outside the box. Thinking outside Congress gets you there.

Serious cuts must be made. Deep cuts. No smoke and mirrors. Restructuring is not about convening to debate whether Program A and Program B and Program C are good, or bad. It is about two columns of numbers, which must be brought into balance. If you don't do that, you haven't restructured. No pretending entitlement programs are some kind of fiscal ghost that's there but can't be seen on a balance sheet. Same way with wars and any other expenditure that gets an "emergency" label and therefore—even if we are talking billions of dollars— is not counted as real money. If you want U.S.A. Inc. to be a serious outfit, you have to draw up a serious balance sheet. Revenues and expenditures are not really a difficult concept unless you are lying— listing imaginary assets when seeking a loan, or hiding real assets when liquidating. If revenues and expenditures balance, you have a going concern. If not, the levees eventually are going to break. The fiscal flood plain extends to every address in the United States, and no insurance is available. Only sanity will keep us all dry. The choice is between real pain now, or suffering a lot more pain later—or rather, passing the pain to your grandkids.

This book is not about giving you my opinions as to which federal employees should be sent home, which programs should be shut down, which wars should be fought, which planets we should visit, or how much security should be provided by Social Security and to which senior citizens. As you no doubt expect, I have some strong opinions about these things. So do you. This is a democracy. So even though both of us would like our country to achieve fiscal sanity, this chapter is not my personal list of line item budget vetoes. It is instead, as M. Scott Peck wrote in the foreword to *Bankrupt*, a plea for sanity. There is no happy ending to the chapter, because the Constitution of the United States does not allow you, or me, or a Debt Czar to take control of the nation's checkbook, even for a moment. That's the bad news. The good news is also the illogical and infuriating news that even as nothing is being done, we do know what has to be done. And there is the further good news I mentioned early on...well, old news actually...that our society used to live in the present rather than the future. So we know it can be done. Maybe, just maybe, our society will get turned back toward fiscal sanity...and maybe, just maybe, Congress will respond in kind... and maybe, just maybe, this can happen before all the wheels come off.

Nothing wrong with a wish list, even for a realist like myself. At the moment I would be happy to see U.S.A. Inc. achieve even an economist's idea of a good balance sheet. I'm not sure—see the Peterson Foundation Survey—most Americans, including our news media, understand how far we must go to reach even that watered-down target. I'm just a turnaround guy who for years has told his debt-drowning clients: "Today is the Tomorrow you worried about Yesterday." I'm not going to sue Paul Volcker for saying: "Today's concerns may soon become tomorrow's existential crises."

10

The Court of Last Resort

*"A person who can't pay gets another person
who can't pay to guarantee that he can pay.
Like a person with two wooden legs getting
another person with two wooden legs to
guarantee that he has got two natural legs.
It don't make either of them able to do a
walking-match."*
— Mr. Pancks in *Little Dorrit*, by Charles Dickens.

Simplicity is the ultimate sophistication.
— Attributed to Leonardo da Vinci.

G overnment has been a complex monstrosity for
so long that no one now alive remembers when
government was simple. It grows still more complex
every year, to the point that quality control at the
ballot box begins to look impossible. Term limits, for
example, make sense—until you realize officeholders
would be shoved out the door just as they began to
understand the basics. Not imposing term limits
makes sense—until you realize officeholders' top
priority has become job security...their own job

security. More and more time is spent raising
campaign money and less and less time is devoted to
governing. No wonder the simplest and most basic
element of good government—fiscal integrity—has
taken more and more of a beating.

Most Americans, I think, understand that their
government has become an inefficient, bureaucratic
swamp. I think Americans understand we are in
deep trouble as a result. I think most citizens are
aware, whether in generality or in serious detail,
that our big entitlement programs alone are on track
to bankrupt us. I think it's all overwhelming for the
average citizen. Warning about a debt-driven public
policy disaster, as I have tried to do with my two
books, is a bit like walking along the San Andreas
Fault, knocking on doors, and announcing: "The
Big Quake is coming." For sure, the comparisons
are striking. What lies ahead in either case is not
pretty, and most people know about the danger. But
in truth there is no comparison.

Nothing can be done to stop the Big Quake. It
could happen a century or two or three down the
road. Unless a Californian wants to take up a new
life in, say, North Dakota, he might as well kick his
earthquake worries on down the road, because the
Big One will cause the same carnage whether it
happens tomorrow or 300 years from now.

The debt bomb, meanwhile, not only can be
defused, it would be a simple task. Painful, but
simple. We don't know exactly when the debt bomb
will do us in, but our current fiscal behavior could
sink us tomorrow night if a perfect storm of financial

events blew into town. Experts already are charting the day Washington will be spending more money on debt service than anything else in the budget. And unlike the Big Quake, the sooner we get serious about fiscal reality the less damage and pain we'll sustain trying to live in the future by raiding our grandchildren's bank accounts.

One of my own grandchildren tells me I should quit worrying about these things. Every generation, he assures me, will meet new challenges and rise to defeat them. I admire and appreciate the young man's spirit when he says: "That'll be for us to take care of, Gramps." He is correct about our country, in its short history, having survived wars and formidable crises. It's also true the next great challenge could be bigger than the last great challenge. It's also true that the bloodiest battlefields are littered with corpses—from both winning and losing sides—who began the day as soldiers confident of victory.

I believe my grandson is on the right track with his implication that Americans have courage, and have a history of doing what it takes to get things done. But I also believe—also know—that paying taxes used to be a matter of pride, a sign of a prosperous citizen pulling his weight in a prosperous and fiscally sane nation. That has all gone away, largely on the same freight that brought the overspending, unrestrained, unfocused, living-in-the-future style of government to town...and then grew it and grew it until you will be hard-pressed to find anyone saying "I am proud to pay my taxes." More often nowadays it's simply "I pay my taxes," a basic statement of legal compliance.

It's difficult to be proud of helping to finance so much waste.

That's a big reason the spending side of Washington's balance sheet must be adjusted first. It's not just because most of the balance-sheet repair will have to come from the spending side. It's also because if Americans see their government getting realistic about how tax dollars are spent...if they see a more responsible Congress...then they will be willing (maybe even proud) to pay increased taxes to reel Washington out of the future and back into the present. If a tax surcharge were specified to be for a certain period of years and dedicated entirely to paying down the debt, while the remainder of taxes supported a balanced budget, that would almost certainly put some pride back in citizenship. Especially if government made an "I am a debtaholic" admission and specified that giving future generations room to breathe would henceforth be official policy.

No doubt a "debtaholic" admission means the simple solution will not happen. Could a majority of Congress ever be prodded into stepping forward and saying: "Guess what? Even if the economy came roaring back, it would not lift us out of this bottomless sinkhole. We are looking at an endless future of federal budget deficits, an endless future of borrowing. Your tax dollars will be spent on interest just like a credit-card junkie. It's our fault, and we don't feel good about that. So we are going to become fiscal realists." In truth, at some point our elected leaders will have no choice. By then, of course, our fiscal situation will have deteriorated so badly that no one could possibly be proud to pay their taxes. Which is putting it charitably.

So to whom—or to what mechanism—do we make this plea? We want our government to act now. Pretend that the largest conglomerate on Earth has a financial officer and needs to pay attention to what he or she says. Make 20 percent cuts across the board in all departments and programs. Send home one in five federal employees (including, of course, congressional staffers). Make adjustments in benefits and "legacy" costs so as to bring government employee reality in line with private-sector employee reality. Announce that never again will the United States borrow even one dollar to pay interest on its debt. Use modern communications media and bring us all into the moral equivalent of a town hall. Make sure every American understands the past of our entitlement programs and the present of our entitlement programs. Show why—as much as we might despair—it is impossible not to make adjustments in the future of our entitlement programs. Drive the spending side of the federal balance sheet straight down below the revenue side, so you can say with a straight face that you might do something about our rusting infrastructure or work on finding a replacement for fossil fuel. Show that Washington, honest as the day is long, will begin living within its means.

That's the case we need to make in the court of last resort. Heaven help us all—even my courageous grandson—if we don't get before that court and win the proper verdict. Otherwise, insanity will rule the day.

The bad news is that Pogo, as I am so fond of saying, had it right. If we want to meet the enemy, all we have to do is look in the mirror. The good news is that the true court of last resort is also us. We can reverse ourselves. Even a bloated, immobile, debt-buried government will have to respond if presented with a clear, strong, unmistakable judgment from the people. We want to live in the present, we want to live within our means, we want to stop robbing our grandchildren. We want fiscal integrity to be government policy.

If that clear judgment came down, it would be my great pleasure to declare that Pogo finally got one wrong.

Afterword

David L. Littmann

Senior Economist, Mackinac Center for Public Policy,
Retired Senior Vice-President and Chief Economist,
Comerica Bank, Detroit.

June 5, 2010

One decade into the 21st Century, many millions of Americans are not poor, but are impoverished of spirit. They are not stupid, but are uncommonly ignorant. Are they "living in some future financial utopia," rather than in the real world, as Jim McTevia thoroughly nails it? No doubt.

What can be done about our nation's fiscal trajectory toward bankruptcy and the obliteration of wealth?

No one I've ever met has had more experience than Jim McTevia in the psychology and financial techniques required for pulling individuals, families, or enterprises away from the financial brink. Indeed, nearly half a century ago McTevia and a bare handful of pathfinders scattered across the country invented the turnaround management profession, now practiced by thousands from coast to coast. Their clients include practically every type of business.

Jim McTevia is no politician. Trendy, politically correct doctrines have no constructive role to play in his ministry of renewed fiscal life or his pronouncement of financial death to management and owners. Armed with experience and objective analysis of traditional accounting statements, he can assess instantly whether clients and prospects have passed the point of no return or if, by swift, corrective, and often quite painful behavioral changes, the entity is salvageable as a going concern. It's a beautiful thing to bring a business back from the edge of an apparently irremediable situation.

This is the guts of McTevia's message here: America's existential threat—an entire nation staring into that same fiscal abyss!

Today's budgeting chaos—headlined globally by Greek fiscal turmoil and by escalating U.S. insolvency at every level of government—is case in point. The common thread is a spendthrift mindset (a willful recklessness) with which inhabitants of these lands live their lives far beyond their means, expecting the same of their public officials in school districts, municipalities, states, and Washington. Government budgeting thereby becomes an extension of irresponsible constituent behavior. In every instance, modern citizens have broken the moral code by living at the expense of future generations. The crime is "intergenerational theft."

Franklin, Hamilton, and Jefferson all saw this coming and implored our Republic's voters and legislators to do all in their power to avoid this most selfish and ultimately corrupting temptation. Thomas Jefferson put it most succinctly in a letter he wrote in 1816: "I sincerely believe that the principle of spending money to be paid by posterity under the name of funding is but swindling futurity on a large scale."

Why would a nation whose forefathers bore such immense peacetime and wartime burdens, sacrificed so much in terms of toil and material well-being, and never knew but a fraction of the choices, liberties, and luxuries enjoyed by current generations... make decisions to engage in such sustained, profligate financial activity? A twofold answer: First, economic incentives to behave in fiscally unjustifiable ways have been embedded in legislation and exacerbated by legislators for many decades. Second, all governmental accounting is incredibly deficient in one basic way—it lacks the all-important balance sheet that constitutes an entire set of financial statements requiring a dedicated stream of existing revenues to cover deficits, borrowings, and debts, and assuring defeasance of these debts via sinking funds.

The good news is that both fundamental flaws in our nation's financial behavior lend themselves to permanent fixes. But do Americans have the willpower and energy to demand corrective legislation that restores our fiscal integrity? Do we have the resolve to implement real financial change that revives political stability, military credibility, and economic dynamism in the global arena?

Incentives:

The corrective action for missing incentives is to restore them. When legislators extended unemployment benefits from 26 to 39 to 79 weeks (and by June 2010 proposed 99 weeks!), it came as no surprise to anyone possessing even a scintilla of economic sense that such extensions would lead the average unemployed individual to remain unemployed longer. Even Larry Summers, top economic advisor to the president—before turning politician—had written that unemployed people begin their serious job searches four weeks before job benefits expire. Sure enough, by mid-2010, the average length of unemployment per laid-off worker had already reached its highest point in U.S. economic history. Answer: Terminate extended benefits that are paid with borrowed funds and by higher taxes on people barely able to keep their own jobs.

An example of inverted incentives is the mandate to raise minimum wages and benefits, regardless of corresponding worker productivity. It is axiomatic that such political overrides of the competitive marketplace result in major destruction of jobs and massive loss of benefits to remaining workers. Among the latest example is the loss of 2,000 fishing-industry jobs in American Samoa (a U.S. possession). Answer: remove minimum-wage legislation. Politicians, despite so-called stimulus funds, haven't the money to pay higher wages and benefits. They must borrow from the future.

Therefore, defeating lethal incentives is no different than attacking virulent cancers. Essentially, the technique for destroying "moral hazards" is to remove them altogether. Out-of-control spending must be quarantined, identified, and killed. Absent such discipline and resolve, the patient dies. Moreover, to prevent a re-emergence of the spending disease, legislative perpetrators must be removed from office; their behaviors must be investigated and (where necessary) prosecuted for violations of public trust of sworn oaths to uphold, defend, and protect the Constitution.

Government Balance Sheet:

In the private sector, no successful business survives without daily reference to its two vital financial touchstones: the profit and loss statement and the balance sheet. In contrast, governments blithely reference only their spending and revenue statement. They see roughly how much is spent on government programs and how much they collect. When spending exceeds income, governments resort to higher, more destructive taxes and spending from their euphemistic "rainy day fund."

What they lack is a balance sheet—an explicit statement of assets (what's owned) and liabilities (what's owed). Thus, governments automatically ignore the basic responsibility of providing funds necessary to cover expenses associated with depreciation and upkeep of owned assets such as office buildings, military complexes, parks and monuments. Just as bad, when times turn tough for the private sector, governments have no organized means of liquidating (selling) surplus and uneconomical facilities (land, structures and equipment) to buyers, domestically or internationally. They lack the symmetry of accounting structures found in the disciplined, competitive marketplace.

For this reason, Social Security, Medicare, Medicaid, ObamaCare (not to mention public employee pension and health-care programs and dozens more) are ticking time bombs. Need proof?

Consider the fact that Washington actually made money on the purchase of many homes and businesses at distressed prices during 2008 and 2009. The U.S. Treasury paid mere cents on the dollar to acquire homes and properties whose values subsequently rose in 2010. By selling these assets at higher prices in 2010, a proper government accounting would have dedicated the proceeds to paying down debt incurred in the initial purchases. Instead, having no balance sheet to acknowledge or account for what it had done, Washington simply *spent* the proceeds from its sales, rather than dedicating the "profits" to the payoff of the debt incurred when it borrowed or printed money to finance its activity.

Answer: Create a balance sheet, complete with a sinking fund or capital account that dedicates revenues to a paydown of debt and provides fully for depreciation. Until this basic financial aberration is rectified, government fiscal integrity cannot be maintained at any level for long. Like the law of gravity, proper accounting applies ubiquitously to every firm, household, and government.

Ironically, the final and perhaps seminal thought of this Afterword may well be captured in the masterful title of Jim McTevia's prior book, *Bankrupt: A Society Living in the Future*. On June 5, 2010, a *Wall Street Journal* editorial stated the likelihood that our nation's sole remaining option for averting a financial meltdown will be for local and state units of government to petition for court bankruptcies that would abrogate (thereby reopening to negotiation) ruinous public sector contracts. California and New Jersey are already at the default stage and contemplating these alternatives.

Hats off to Jim McTevia for having provided the fiscal bible, proper focus, and accurate predictions of coming problems and solutions. He did so two decades before the rest of the crowd recognized either the scope or inevitability of both the problem and resolution.

Acknowledgments

Without a doubt the events that occurred beginning in late 2008 were largely the main reason for this book. Earlier, I thought I would send a letter, manuscript or some such communication to my grandchildren, perhaps in the guise of a legacy or holiday gift along with the usual holiday check. I sought out my friend and editor, Tom Ferguson, from the publication of my earlier book, *BANKRUPT: A Society Living in the Future*, to help me craft some form of document. However, as the events unfolded, I was astounded by the accuracy of my prediction in *BANKRUPT*. Tom was adamant that the real legacy for my grandchildren and all the other grandchildren of my friends and fellow Americans was to once again attempt to reach a forum for my belief of the financial Armageddon that I was certain our society was headed for. I owe Tom my deepest gratitude for his insistence and support.

However, my greatest appreciation is to the hundreds of clients and families whose lives I touched over the last 50 years during a time of stress through events that, according to psychologists, is second only to the death of a loved one. Their stories and the choices they made to live far in the future gained me the experience to write this book.

As the draft of this book took form, I invited my friend and highly regarded economist, David

Littmann, for his opinions and comments and then contacted my former publisher, Bill Haney, to let him know what was underway. Both David and Bill reviewed the earlier chapters. Bill was insistent of the importance of the book and the message it sent. He stepped in immediately and took over the publishing and marketing. What a privilege to have the support and guidance of such a well-known and highly respected media expert. Bill has authored numerous books and his willingness to publish this book was an honor. Thanks, David and Bill.

I am convinced my success in the highly specialized field I practice in is largely a result of the support of my many associates over the years. This is particularly true of my two longest associates, Joanne Vancour and Kathleen Pietrzak. So I invited them, along with my newest associate, my granddaughter Maggie, to review, comment and critique earlier chapters. Their efforts and their contributions prove yet again that no one in life becomes successful on their own. My thanks to each of you.

As the manuscript neared completion, no one was comfortable with the title I had chosen: "The Grandchild Thieves". We considered more than fifty titles, but only after my wife selected *THE CULTURE OF DEBT,* were we all satisfied. Thank you, Joan, for the gift of a great title.

Jim McTevia
Harbor Springs, Michigan
July 26, 2010